I0558160

SOCIAL SKILLS FOR TEENS

How to Build Confidence, Strong Communication Skills, and Become Your Best Self

Jamie Myers

ISBN: 978-1-957590-38-7

For questions, email: Support@AwesomeReads.org

Please consider writing a review!

Just visit: AwesomeReads.org/review

FREE BONUS

SCAN TO GET OUR NEXT BOOK FOR FREE!

TABLE OF CONTENTS

INTRODUCTION

Teenagers today are grappling with a mix of unique challenges and opportunities brought on by the ever-evolving landscape of technology and social media. They benefit from the privilege of having a wealth of information at their fingertips, yet they contend with the complexities of virtual relationships and the scourge of online bullying.

In this fast-paced, rapidly changing world, social skills have never been more crucial to forming healthy relationships, communicating effectively, and navigating a myriad of interpersonal obstacles. Social skills are essential for promoting well-being, resilience, and success for this generation, whether with family, peers, or the wider community. This book includes basic guidelines for making friends, information on building meaningful relationships in person and online, and three chapters on how teens can create balance between their responsibilities and relationships.

CHAPTER ONE: WHAT ARE SOCIAL SKILLS?

Social skills are an essential component of the human experience, and they play a critical role in shaping our lives. They're the foundation for how we interact with others, form relationships, and navigate the complexities of daily life. It's especially important to develop good social skills as a teenager since they play an integral part in how you develop your identity and navigate the world.

Your teenage years can be a time of great change and uncertainty. Strong social skills are essential while you're establishing your independence, testing the waters of social relationships, and facing new challenges.

One of the key elements of social skills is the ability to communicate effectively. Communication is at the heart of all relationships, and you need to be able to express yourself clearly and concisely. Good communication skills also involve active listening, empathy, and the ability to understand the perspectives of others.

The Definition of Social Skills

The word *social* refers to relationships and interactions between individuals in a social setting, such as with family, peers, or a wider community. This term encompasses the skills and behaviors necessary for effective communication, building positive relationships, and navigating social situations with confidence and resilience. Social skills play a critical role in shaping your sense of self, maintaining your mental health and well-being, and setting a strong foundation for your future success.

Studies have shown that people thrive when they can relate to others and make a positive impact in their communities. As a teenager, contributing to your social groups is one of the most important tasks you can do. By cultivating social skills, you can provide deeper emotional and practical support to your loved ones.

Adolescence is actually a prime time for giving back to others. With so many changes happening in your brain, you have the cognitive, emotional, and physical capabilities to make significant contributions that benefit those around you. Altruism, in turn, helps you develop the qualities you need to succeed in adulthood.

What Does It Mean to Be Social?

Being social doesn't just refer to having an extroverted personality; it revolves around actively engaging in social interactions and intentionally building meaningful relationships. There are many ways to do that. This could involve participating in social events, talking with friends and family, forming new relationships, and connecting with online and in-person groups. Socializing is a key aspect of ordinary human life. It's how you connect with others, and it can affect your well-being, happiness, and sense of belonging.

Social interactions play a crucial role in human development, especially during the teenage years. Whether you're introverted, new to a school, or just learning how to communicate with others, it's important to develop some key skills. Selecting compatible friends and approaching them to form a team is the first step. Here are some ways to maintain a social lifestyle:

- Making and maintaining healthy friendships
- Working effectively with peers and teachers
- Participating in extracurricular activities
- Exploring job opportunities
- Building a supportive network of peers and adults at school, clubs, and beyond

- Maintaining strong mental health and positive self-esteem
- Leading positive change in your community

Why Being Social Is Part of Growing Up

So many traits that keep adults going today were established during their teen years; without a doubt, building a strong foundation of social skills and relationships is a goal that's worth pursuing. This isn't just because you want to avoid peer pressure or bullying. It's also to ensure you can remain your best self as you grow up.

Having supportive relationships with relatives, schoolmates, and peers plays a major role in your emotional well-being and academic success. Building strong social connections is crucial to help you relate to those you spend the most time with. If you struggle with being shy or experience social anxiety, there are ways to overcome it, such as practicing conversations with siblings or even using the mirror.

As a teenager, you may want to be independent and make your own decisions, but having healthy relationships with friends, siblings, and parents can provide support during this stage. Interacting with classmates and others will not only improve your communication skills but also help you develop empathy. By interacting with your friends, you may learn about their family and relationship histories, which can provide insight into how to better

6

appreciate people for who they are. These lessons will stay with you throughout your life.

PRACTICE AND PATIENCE: SKILLS TAKE TIME

Let's talk about self-improvement. Who doesn't want to be the best version of themselves? But sometimes it's hard to know where to start. Do you need to work on your public speaking, social skills, or navigating social media? It's important to figure out your goals first. There are different ways to learn depending on the skill you want to develop and your personal style, but there are some basic principles you should keep in mind to make progress. The key is to approach self-improvement in a strategic and mindful way. Taking the time to think about your goals and plan your approach will pay off in a big way. Let's get started!

Check Your Readiness

When you're learning a new skill or trying to get better at something, there are two important questions to ask yourself. First, is your goal something that you can realistically achieve? And second, how much time and effort are you willing to put in to reach that goal? It's not always easy to improve yourself, but it's important to understand that learning a new skill takes time and effort. It doesn't mean you're not talented or skilled already. In fact, it's quite the opposite—it shows that you're willing to put in the work to become even better.

Make Sure Your Goals Are Relevant

I recommend picking a social skill that's connected to your future career or interests. Sure, public speaking may seem cool, but ask yourself if it will really help you in the long run. Learning a new skill takes time and effort, so it's important to know what you'll get out of it before diving in. Once you've decided which skill to focus on first, you should also figure out the best way to learn it.

Understand What Motivates You to Learn

Everyone has their own unique way of learning! Some people might learn best by looking at pictures or reading, while others would rather watch videos or hear explanations. You might even need to get your hands dirty and experience things firsthand.

It's a good idea to reflect on your past experiences and figure out what works best for you. This will keep you on track toward learning something new or achieving a goal. Make a list of the times when you really excelled and when you struggled. Did the successful experiences have anything in common? What about the negative ones? By identifying what works and what doesn't, you can find out which factors help you the most and then seek out ways to create that optimal learning environment. It could be as simple as finding a tutor or study group, or maybe you need to make a schedule for yourself to help you make consistent progress. Even just keeping a journal or log of your efforts can help keep you accountable to yourself. The key is never giving up on yourself and always exploring new ways to learn!

Get the Right Help

Learning a new skill can be tough, but it's so much easier when you've got someone to help you out. And who better to learn from than someone who's already a pro at it? If you want to learn how to budget your money, for example, find an adult you trust who's good at managing their finances. They can show you how to save, when to spend, and how to keep track of everything. Seeking out this help is much easier than trying to do it alone, and the interaction will double as a way to practice your social skills.

You might be wondering who you can ask for help. Well, think about the people you look up to: your guardian, a teacher, a coach, or even an older sibling. You want to choose someone who's patient, understanding, and good at explaining things. You should feel comfortable talking to them. You don't have to choose only one person either. If there's someone who gives good advice and another person who explains thing well, you can receive advice from the first person and ask the second person questions to clarify.

Start Small

Learning a new skill can be hard, right? It can feel like you have to do everything at once, and that can be overwhelming. But the truth is that you can't do everything at once, and if you try, you might not get anywhere. Here's what you can do instead: Pick one or two social skills you want to improve and focus on them first. Then break them down into small, achievable goals. Let's say you want to be more assertive. A good first step would be to practice speaking up more in class. Maybe you want to be the first person to answer a question or add your input into classroom discussion. This will require you to study the material in advance and reflect on your opinions before class. That will make it easier to express what you think about the subject when the opportunity arises. Start with that and build on it. Remember: You got this!

Reflect Along the Way

If you want to get better at something, it's important to reflect on what you're learning. Think about what you're doing well and what you need to improve on. This will help you move from just trying something out to really mastering it. It's a good idea to keep a journal and dedicate it to taking notes about what works for you and what you find challenging.

Another helpful practice is to talk to other people. It's good to share your goals with people who can give you helpful feedback and support, even if they don't know all the answers. They can still encourage you to keep going and help you stay on track. And when you talk about your progress, it can be really motivating and make you feel good about the changes you're making. Plus, it keeps you accountable and honest about how you're doing.

Challenge Yourself by Teaching Others

Did you know that one of the fastest ways to learn something new is to teach it to someone else? It's true! So why not share what you've learned with your siblings, guardians, friends, or even your neighbors? Not only will you get to show off your skills, but you'll also solidify your own understanding of the topic.

Here's an idea: Put a "teaching" date on your calendar, or plan to lead a training session a few months from now. This doesn't need to be anything formal; it can simply be a commitment to talk about what you're learning with a person you trust. This will help you stay accountable and keep you motivated. When you have a specific objective in mind, your learning will be much more focused and practical. Plus, you'll be able to share your knowledge with others and gain valuable face-to-face time holding close conversations.

Teaching others is a great way to build confidence and social skills. When you're able to explain something clearly and effectively, you'll feel more self-assured and capable, so don't be afraid to step up and share your expertise. Who knows? You may even discover a passion for teaching or mentoring others.

Be Patient

When we try to learn something new, we usually envision ourselves mastering it quickly, but the truth is that it takes a lot of time and effort to really get good at something. Don't grow discouraged if you don't see immediate progress; studies show that it can take at least six months to develop a new skill. It might take even longer for others to recognize your progress, so don't let that hold you back. In fact, only a small number of people will notice the changes you make. You should focus on your own goals and not worry about what others think. If you're working on learning a new skill, just remember that it takes time, patience, and a lot of hard work. Keep pushing yourself, and soon enough, you'll be a master!

CHAPTER TWO: INTERACTING WITH OTHERS

It's important to have good friends in your life. They can make you feel good about yourself, help you discover new interests, and give you someone to lean on. But building friendships as a teen can be tricky, especially if you're shy, have moved to a new school, or are simply unsure how to talk to people.

That's why it's important to have a few skills under your belt. First, you need to choose the right people to be friends with. Look for those who share similar interests and values as you. Once you find people you'd like to hang out with, you need to approach them and work on building a lasting friendship. It's all about taking the first step and reaching out.

The way you build friendships will change as you become a teen. You might find that you have less in common with old friends or that you're interested in new things. That's okay! It's a part of growing up and discovering who you are. Just remember to be open, honest, and kind to others. With a little bit of effort, you can build strong, meaningful friendships that will last a lifetime.

UNDERSTANDING WHEN THE RIGHT TIME IS

Your friends play a huge role in your life and can impact how you feel about yourself and the world around you. It's totally normal to want to keep your friendships strong, but things can get complicated. You might start to feel like something's off or notice that you're not as close as you used to be. At times, people just drift apart or relationships turn toxic.

So, if you feel like your friendships could use some work, it might be a good idea to evaluate what makes a good friendship and recognize some red flags indicating that a friendship might not be right for you anymore. If you find that your current friends aren't the best fit for you anymore, don't worry! It's never too late to make new friends. In fact, it can be really fun and exciting to meet new people who share your interests and values.

When seeking out new friends, it's important to evaluate how much time you have to devote to spending with new people. Having healthy boundaries in mind will keep you from overloading your schedule or neglecting other responsibilities such as family or schoolwork. Another thing to keep in mind is that not every occasion is appropriate for building social skills. Although you can make friends in class, it's not a good choice to socialize during a lesson or while people are studying. It's better to wait until breaks, during lunch, or after class to practice these skills.

This same concept should be applied to conversations. While it's great to start conversations with new people, some times are better than others for doing so. If two people are already engaged in a conversation, it's best to wait until they're finished talking before joining. It's not a good idea to interrupt conversations or intrude on an activity where someone is trying to focus. Learning how to identify when the appropriate time to engage with others will take some trial and error.

If this is something that seems confusing or difficult, it's a good idea to have test conversations with a trusted adult. The same thing goes for deciding how much time you have to devote to social interactions. Talking to your guardians about your responsibilities at home and expectations for school may help you decide how many hours a week you have to spend on making new friends and maintaining established relationships.

CAN YOU BE YOURSELF?

Real friends accept you just the way you are. You should feel comfortable being yourself when you're with them—whether that means wearing your favorite outfit, sharing your thoughts, or talking about your hobbies. It's important to ask yourself if you feel accepted around your friends or if you have to act like someone you're not whenever you're with them.

It's a good idea to pay attention to anyone who makes you feel small, guilty, or insecure. This is a sign that they're not the right person for you to socialize with. A good friend won't be offended if you can't hang out because you have to study or do chores. Likewise, a good friend will want to see you succeed and will celebrate your accomplishments rather than trying to compete with you.

Are Your Friends Listening to You?

Your friends should care about you and want to know what you're thinking and feeling, so it's important to notice whether they're really listening to you. Pay attention to their body language while you're talking to them. Are they nodding and showing they understand what you're saying? Do they remember your conversations, especially the important ones? If so, that's a sign that they're engaged and care about what you have to say. This is what makes a true friend—someone who is

16

there for you, listens to you, and supports you no matter what. As you practice your social skills, always make sure to surround yourself with friends who truly care about you and your well-being. They should have a healthy investment in your goals, dreams, and needs.

HOW TO BUILD CONFIDENCE

If you're feeling unsure of yourself, it might seem like it's easier to just sit back and not get involved. But here's the thing: Lacking confidence can actually hold you back in a big way. You might feel too nervous to speak up in class, avoid trying new things, or even give in to negative peer pressure. The worst part is that when you don't have confidence, you're more likely to think you'll fail at whatever you try or give up too quickly when things get tough. Fortunately, building up your confidence is something you can totally work on.

Building confidence is key during your teenage years. Being self-confident means you believe in yourself and your worth. It's all about having a positive outlook about yourself and your abilities. When you've got that self-assurance, you trust your own decisions, skills, and talents. This helps you set goals and stay true to your beliefs as you expand your social network. Plus, when you're confident, you're better equipped to handle all the wild ups and downs of being a teenager.

Avoid Negativity

Let's face it — no one has time for that. It's important to love and respect yourself enough to let go of things that make you unhappy. So, if you're dealing with something that's hurting you, take a step back and focus on things that bring you joy instead. But how do you avoid negative energy?

Take a break from social media if it's causing you stress or making you feel bad about yourself. While it can be entertaining, it can also be pretty harmful. Instead, try doing things you enjoy, such as taking a walk, reading a book, or hanging out with friends and family.

Let go of unhealthy relationships. I know it's hard, but if someone is always putting you down or making you feel terrible about yourself, it might be time to move on and find healthier relationships.

Start Journaling

Journaling can do wonders for your confidence by helping you clear your thoughts or make better decisions. Plus, it's a great way to give yourself some well-deserved compliments! One good way to use journaling to build your confidence is by recording your accomplishments, happy moments, and everything you are grateful for in your life. The act itself can help improve your confidence, and on bad days it gives you something to look back on and remember. By looking at old accomplishments, you can also see where you've grown and what things you've overcome. It's easy to take progress for granted. Keeping

18

a record of the journey can help you maintain a positive perspective.

Take Care of Your Physical and Mental Health

Feeling good physically and mentally is key to building confidence. Of course, you can't expect to feel great about yourself if you're not taking care of your health. Here are some tips to help you feel your best:

Eat a healthy diet. Nourishing your body with nutritious foods can help you feel more energized and improve your overall physical and mental health.

Get moving and exercise regularly. Physical activity releases endorphins, which are commonly considered happy hormones. Endorphins can help you feel more confident and positive. Exercise, which includes any form of play that raises your heart rate, will also provide a release on bad days. The next time you feel stressed or have a strong emotional response, try doing something active before reacting and see how it feels.

Try meditating to ground yourself. Meditation has been shown to have a ton of health benefits, including boosting self-confidence. You'll learn to live more in tune with your beliefs and goals and feel more centered. There are many short 5- to 10-minute guided meditations available for free online to get you started. If this doesn't sound appealing to you, doing something as simple as sitting outside while you focus on your senses can help ground you and build mindfulness.

Consider talking to a therapist if you struggle with negative thoughts or mental health issues. Therapists can help you learn coping mechanisms and develop healthy habits, which will leave you feeling happier, healthier, and more confident. Having a therapist is a great tool even if you don't have negative thoughts. They can offer guidance and support as you achieve your social goals and provide a confidential ear to reflect on your new friendships or relationships.

In the end, building self-confidence takes some work, but it's totally worth it. Taking care of yourself and focusing on the positive aspects of your life will lead to a happier, more satisfied you.

WAYS TO START A CONVERSATION

Every day, before you even get out of bed, chances are you're already reaching for your phone to check your messages or start new chats with your friends or loved ones. And when you do finally step out into the world, you'll probably run into a mix of familiar and unfamiliar faces, all of whom deserve a friendly "hello" or a quick catch-up on how their day is going. It's commonly considered basic courtesy.

20

Starting a conversation is like rolling the dice — you never quite know what side they're going to land on. Depending on the circumstances, there are all kinds of factors that can influence how a conversation starts. It could be the time of day, the number of people involved, the nature of your relationship, the topic at hand, or the mode and platform of communication. But no matter the circumstances, the key is to find a way to kick off a lively and engaging conversation that leaves everyone feeling good.

How Do You Start a Conversation?

Friends

Starting conversations with potential new friends or friendly acquaintances can be intimidating at times, especially if you're worried about how they might respond to your approach. The first thing to keep in mind is that even if things don't go as planned, that's completely okay. Everyone makes social blunders as they learn and grow, and each attempt will teach you something new. Furthermore, if something doesn't go as planned, it doesn't mean that same approach won't go over well with another person. You're not going to have easy conversations with every person you talk to.

To start a conversation with a friend, asking them questions or giving them a light compliment is usually a safe icebreaker. When giving compliments, it's best to avoid complimenting people's physical attributes and to always make sure the compliment is genuine. For example, you may like their shoes or think their input during class was especially interesting. This can be a great way to lead into asking questions about them. For example, if you like what they said in class, you might ask follow-up questions to continue the conversation or ask them about their study habits. Remember to keep conversations light until you get to know them and learn more about what they're comfortable talking about.

Although it's good to help people learn more about you, it's advisable to limit how much you talk about yourself at first. Let others ask questions, and keep your responses about the same length as theirs to keep the conversation balanced so that you learn about each other equally. Sometimes, people can overshare when they're nervous, and although this is normal behavior, it can make it difficult for the other person to remain engaged and comfortable if you haven't established a bond yet. Likewise, some people might feel overwhelmed if they're given too much information too fast. This can cause them to pull away instead of furthering the conversation.

Strangers

Starting a conversation with a stranger can be uncomfortable, especially when there's no level of familiarity. However, you can start the conversation much like you would when making friends, either by paying them a compliment or calling their attention to something that interests you. Another really great approach is to find similar ground or ask for help. For example, if you're talking to a stranger at a grocery store, it might be because you need help finding something. If

22

you're talking to a stranger at school, you might ask them for directions somewhere or request information on an upcoming school event. If you're attending a sporting activity, you could ask them what they thought about the game or if they know anyone playing. The trick is to look for what you and that stranger have in common.

The key is to be open, friendly, and curious. Even if you're a bit nervous, just remember that most people are happy to have a conversation and make a new connection. By approaching someone with a positive attitude and a genuine interest in what they have to say, you'll be well on your way to striking up a great conversation with a stranger.

Teachers and Mentors

When it comes to starting a conversation with a teacher or mentor, it's important to show them that you respect their time, privacy, and schedule. This means putting their needs ahead of your own and being as polite and direct as possible when making your request. While it's true that you may benefit from the conversation, it's important to remember that they're taking time out of their busy schedule to speak with you. Make sure that you're clear and concise in what you're asking for.

To start off on the right foot, stick to the topic and avoid asking rhetorical questions. This will set the pace for a relevant and productive conversation. And as the conversation progresses, make sure to do more listening than talking. This will show that you're engaged and interested in what they have to say, and it will help you build a stronger rapport with them.

WAYS TO INTRODUCE YOURSELF

Introducing yourself is a key part of making connections and building relationships, and it all starts with knowing the right way to do it. Of course, you don't need to introduce yourself to people who already know you — that would just be awkward! But when you're meeting someone new, it's important to make a good first impression. That's why it's crucial to cover the three basic sections of any introduction.

Who You Are

Just start with a friendly greeting and introduce yourself. You can start by just letting the other person know your name in a way that feels natural. If you have a more appropriate nickname for the context, feel free to use it instead. For example, if you're meeting someone in a casual setting, you might say, "Hi. My name is Samantha, but you can call me Sam."

Another good way to introduce yourself is to provide some background about yourself. For example, you might say something like, "I'm a student at XYZ" or "I play baseball." This gives the other person some context for the conversation and helps establish common ground.

Formal Introductions

When you're introducing yourself in a formal setting, it's important to keep your focus on what you do rather than on any unrelated personal information. Let's say you're a student who likes music and gardening. If you happen to run into another musician who's willing to chat with you for a few minutes, you should focus on your musical background.

You could say, "Hello, my name is [your name]. I study music at X," or you could focus on something more specific like, "I play X instrument for the school band." Some relevant phrases to use when introducing yourself in a formal context might include:

- "I work at [location or company]."
- "I do [secondary job or skill] in my spare time, but my main focus is on [primary job or skill]."
- "I have a few different skills, but I'm most proficient in [primary skill]."
- "I'm focusing on [primary goal or career path] right now."

If you haven't earned any accolades yet, that's perfectly alright! You can always focus on your aspirations. "I am currently working toward studying [interest] at [potential university]" or "I'm aspiring to be a [future career]."

What Your Listener Needs to Know

Remember that your listener doesn't need to know every detail about you right off the bat. Instead, think of the

25

introduction as a way to let them know why you're having the conversation. Some phrases that can help you breeze through this part of the introduction are:

- "Yesterday, we talked about [topic] over the phone."
- "I'm here today to see if we could…"
- "I reached out as soon as I remembered that you…"
- "I thought you would be the best person to…"

Remember that the introduction is just as important as the takeaway, whether it's a casual chat or a more formal interaction. By keeping it brief and to the point, you can set the tone for a productive and engaging discussion that leaves a lasting impression.

CHAPTER THREE: RESPECT ANYONE AND EVERYONE

Respect is a big deal, and you should keep in mind that respect is reciprocal. That means that when you treat others with respect, you're more likely to be respected in return. And let's be real—we all want to be respected, right? Showing respect in communication applies whether your conversation is face to face or virtual.

Unfortunately, the internet has made it way too easy for people to be disrespectful. It's like people think that just because they're behind a screen, they can say whatever they want to whomever they want. And that's a real problem, especially for teens who are just starting to navigate the world of online communication. When you're out in the world, you can't just hide behind your screen. You've got to interact with people directly.

WHAT IS RESPECT AND WHY DOES IT MATTER?

Respect is a fundamental leadership skill and a critical aspect of how you interact with others. It's also super important if you want to build healthy relationships. Respect is all about showing consideration towards yourself and others, and it can involve things like listening, being courteous, valuing other people's opinions, and treating them with dignity and fairness.

When you show respect, you're extending basic decency toward another human. You don't have to like or agree with someone to be respectful. In fact, you can even continue to be respectful through disagreements with people you don't like without sacrificing what you believe in. This is a skill that shows great strength and emotional control when mastered.

At a basic level, respect means recognizing that all humans are different. Strangers, bosses, teachers, family, and friends all have private struggles and insecurities. There's more going on with every person you meet than what you see on the surface. Most people are just trying their best, and you never know what might hurt or offend

28

them, which is why it is good to practice a basic level of courtesy with every person in your life.

How you treat others will also impact your reputation, which refers to how people perceive you and what they say about you to others. If you are nice to your friends but harsh or cruel to people who are different from you, that might leave you with a reputation for being a bully. Aside from the permanent impact that this kind of behavior could have on another individual, it could also tarnish your reputation in the eyes of teachers, possible employers, or even future friends and romantic partners.

Now that we've covered why respect is important and given a basic rundown of what it is, here are some specific examples:

Acceptance: Every person you meet has a right to take up the same amount of space and have the same opportunities as you do. Regardless of how different a person may seem from you, they are still a living, breathing human with feelings, dreams, aspirations, and struggles.

Empathy: It's a good practice to imagine what other people's experiences are like and how you would feel if you were in their position. For example, your teachers most likely have lots of students, some of whom are rude. They have piles of homework to grade for every one of your peers in class. In addition to work, they likely have personal struggles just like you do. Their struggles might not be the same, but they most likely have something in their lives that adds on more stress than what you see in class. Empathy is a powerful tool when it comes to respecting people's time or understanding their point of view during conflicts.

Kindness: Even if you don't like someone, you should still show them a basic level of kindness. Kindness creates an environment that makes life better for everyone. You can show kindness by choosing non-offensive words, being generous when possible, avoiding conversational topics that hurt people or make them uncomfortable, and helping when you can.

Active listening: This is a form of listening that shows the other person you hear them and value what they are saying. Ways you can demonstrate active listening include maintaining eye contact, asking meaningful questions that illustrate you were paying attention, and summarizing what was said.

Taking responsibility: It's normal to make mistakes sometimes; that's how you learn. When you make a mistake or offend someone, though, it's important to take responsibility and apologize as soon as you recognize where you went wrong.

Gratitude: Saying thank you and giving credit where it's due will go a long way toward showing others respect. Thanking people for holding open a door or helping you on a project shows them that you respect the time and energy they put into making your life a little easier.

Keeping promises: It's a good habit to avoid promising anything if you aren't sure you can deliver. If someone asks you to do something or participate, and you're

30

uncertain you can follow through, you can always say, "I appreciate the offer, but I need to check my schedule before committing to that."

Gossiping and secrets: When possible, avoid sharing secrets or gossiping about someone who isn't present in the conversation. It's best to stop gossip before you hear it, and you can do that by simply saying, "I understand you mean well, but I would rather talk about something else if that's okay." If someone wants to tell you a secret, make sure you're willing to keep their confidence before you hear it. If someone tells you anything about themselves, it's best not to repeat it. If you're uncertain about how private the information is, ask immediately, even if it's something small: "Is this something you want kept private, or is it okay to ask [another person] for help?"

Self-care: Self-respect is just as important as respecting others. This means valuing your time, opinions, and needs as much as you would those of another person. If you wouldn't talk to someone you love the way you talk to yourself, then you're not showing yourself the respect you deserve. It's important that you show yourself the same kindness and compassion you give to others.

DON'T JUDGE PEOPLE BASED ON HOW THEY LOOK

As animals, humans are hardwired to subconsciously pick up on cues in their environment regarding potential threats. Sometimes, this can lead us to hold harmful beliefs about specific groups of people. A whimsical but real example might be cartoon or fairytale witches. These are often depicted as older women, sometimes with a hooked nose with a wart and a deep, cackling laugh. Children might be afraid of anyone who looked like these make-believe characters and hold harmful judgments toward older people. This is a common example of a judgment a child might make, but the ones you experience are probably far different and subtler. It could be anything from someone's hairstyle to how they are eating their lunch, and it's important to not only become aware of these internal judgments but also remind yourself that there is a whole person behind that one attribute you feel uncomfortable with.

Although first impressions are important, it's ideal to give people the benefit of the doubt and allow them an opportunity to show you who they really are. Even if someone comes off a little rude the first time you meet them, they may just be having a bad day. A person could seem like they are being stand-offish or cold toward you when they're really just shy. They might warm up to you on the second or third interaction. Just like you wouldn't want people to only remember how you showed up on your worst day, you should allow people the same opportunity before deciding what you think and feel about them.

At the most basic level, you want to treat people with the same respect you would want in return. No matter how hard you try, everyone will have at least one thing that they dislike about you in some way. It'll be something different from person to person. For example, your sibling may get annoyed by a certain phrase you use, while your friends think that same saying is charming. Your teacher might be annoyed by how you doodle in class, whereas your mother absolutely loves your artwork. With this in mind, you wouldn't want people to only see the one thing they don't like and be completely oblivious to who you are as a whole. That's why it's so important to look past initial judgments when getting to know someone.

WAYS TO SHOW KINDNESS TO EVERYONE

There are many ways to spread compassion and kindness to the people around you. Whether it's your classmates, family, or friends, you have the power to brighten someone's day and lift their spirits with little effort. Here are a few ideas on how you can show kindness in simple ways:

Smile at others: A genuine smile will not only help improve your mood but also the moods of those around you. Even when speaking on the phone, people can often hear the difference between someone who's smiling and someone who isn't.

Be grateful: Gratitude is a powerful tool that can help you combat negative thoughts and show other people you appreciate them. When someone does something nice for you, take a moment to express your appreciation. It makes them feel good and could also inspire them to be more grateful themselves. It's contagious—when you see how much your gratitude can impact others, you'll want to keep spreading the love.

Offer to help someone: It may seem intimidating to offer your help, especially if you feel you don't have much to give. If you feel awkward offering your help, start small' and casual. Opening doors for people, helping pick up items someone dropped, cleaning up trash in public areas, or asking your parents if there's anything they would like help with are good places to start. Although it's nice to help people, it's important to avoid overextending yourself. This means only offering to help when your schedule and energy levels allow. It should never feel like a burden or create a sense of resentment.

Give an honest compliment: Compliments are amazing mood boosters! Next time you're out and about, try spreading some positivity by giving someone a sincere compliment. You never know how much of an impact it could make. It might be as simple as telling your friend that their new haircut looks awesome or telling a stranger that their outfit is on point. Seeing someone light up with a smile will make you feel great too!

34

Give a gift: Giving a gift is a great way to show someone how much you care about them, and it doesn't have to be expensive. A short note, a flower, or a handmade craft are all inexpensive ways to show that you appreciate someone. Gift giving can also transform into a fun form of self-care amongst friends. Surrounding yourself with people who reciprocate the same kindness as you can be a nourishing and fun experience.

These are just a few examples of how you can show kindness to those around you and in your society. As much as it's important to be kind to others, you also need to be kind to yourself.

CHAPTER FOUR: USING HUMOR EFFECTIVELY

You've probably heard that laughter is the best medicine. When people say this, they mean that laughter has positive benefits on our mental, emotional, and physical health. Science has linked stress to a myriad of long-term health issues, and laughter is a way we can combat that stress in our everyday lives. It can even increase productivity during work and school projects because we're more likely to think clearly if we're relaxed.

Although there are exceptions, many people gravitate toward lighthearted and open individuals. It's not a conscious thing; it's just natural for people to want to be happy and avoid discomfort. Many people struggle to feel confident when approaching someone to talk to them for the first time, which is why you're more likely to be approached when you make it easy. This is what we mean when we refer to someone as being "open." We mean that they are easy to talk to on that first encounter. Humor is one way to make yourself approachable.

USING HUMOR TO MAKE FRIENDS

When using humor to make friends, you're creating common ground over something simple and universal—laughter. This is especially great when you are unsure what you and a person have in common. If you feel uncomfortable complimenting them or you don't know what to ask, you can make them laugh and lay the first brick in the foundation of your friendship.

Although we will go into it deeper later in this chapter, it's important to stay positive when making jokes. The perfect starter joke doesn't make fun of or offend anyone. Although you can make jokes at your own expense, self-deprecating humor is tricky and can often slide into something that does more harm than good.

There are many additional subgenres, and comedy can be broken down into a few categories:

Physical humor uses the body. The most iconic symbols associated with physical comedy are the mime and the clown. Pantomiming is when you act something out without words. Traditionally, it's paired with music, but you don't need any to make someone laugh. This can often be silly, and when used properly, a lot of fun. There are many movies you can watch that involve physical comedy for you to study, and the best part is that this activity alone is great for strengthening bonds between friends.

Self-deprecating humor is when someone makes fun of themselves. Although this can be helpful for dealing with embarrassing moments, it's important that you are never actually cruel to yourself. There is a huge difference between not taking yourself too seriously and being mean or bitter to yourself. Usually, you (and other people) can tell the difference by looking at the intention of the joke.

Puns and "dad jokes" are often considered corny; however, if you acknowledge and own this fact, then they can make excellent icebreakers. Puns are a form of wit that uses wordplay to create jokes. Dad jokes are usually clean one-liners. These are great because they are short and punchy. There are books and websites filled with these kinds of jokes. Try searching for and memorizing some for each of your subjects in school (e.g., math, English, or science) and see where they naturally come in handy.

Inside jokes occur with people you've already had a shared experience with; something about that shared experience, which is now a shared memory, may seem funny to those who were there. Inside jokes are often moments that won't make sense to an outside person without a lengthy explanation. It's wonderful to have an inside joke with a friend; however, it is important to have empathy for other people present. You don't want to accidentally exclude other people from the fun.

Deadpan comedy is really funny, but it's a little more difficult to pull off because not everyone will pick up on it. This can also be part of the fun. Deadpan humor is also known as "dry" wit or humor. It's characterized by doing something funny or shocking without displaying emotions or facial expressions. It's best for making ironic comments or even darker observations about society. It's also used to create absurd and silly moments while seemingly remaining serious. There are lots of movies out there to watch as research material.

USING HUMOR TO COPE

Humor can become a fantastic coping mechanism as long as it's not used in a negative way. Finding and creating reasons to laugh is an effective form of self-care. Here are common forms of humor that can help you cope with tough times:

Affiliative humor includes dad jokes and corny puns. Let's say you and your friend are racing bikes and your friend crashes. They're okay, but they're a bit banged up. To cope with the pain and any emotions (e.g., frustration,

40

humiliation, disappointment), you can start cracking jokes to lighten the mood and redirect the focus on something else.

Positive reappraisal is when we find something funny to laugh at in frustrating situations. This can be silly or realistic. For example, let's say you and your crush just broke up. You're with your friends and feeling sad, but you want to lighten the mood and reframe the situation into something more positive. You might make a joke like, "The bad news is [their name] and I are no longer dating. The good news is that I am now free to pursue my actual true love, [insert celebrity here]." You're looking on the bright side of the situation. With practice, it will become natural to find things to crack jokes about.

Sometimes, things just aren't funny. That's okay. We can still seek out humor to help cope. This could be watching a funny movie, seeing a comedy show, listening to a funny podcast, or just spending time with whatever friend gets you laughing the hardest and most often. Laughter helps solidify our connections, distract us from discomfort, and genuinely help us feel better over the long haul.

RESOLVING CONFLICT WITH LAUGHTER

Although using laughter during disagreements takes tact, it can be a helpful tool to master. If you're in a disagreement with a friend or family member, a well-timed joke can help break the tension and put the whole situation into perspective. Most of our day-to-day bickering with our loved ones is usually based on small incidents that are often forgotten within a day, week, or month. These moments can be smoothed over with laughter.

It takes trial and error to learn exactly when a joke will work to ease conflict and when it will make things worse. One way you can avoid things getting worse is by making sure your joke doesn't invalidate the other person. For example, let's say your guardian is stressed out. The house is a mess, and you haven't finished your chores. Their workday was rough, and they are overwhelmed. When they're getting upset, you can use deadpan humor to help break the tension, but it needs to be accompanied by immediate action in order for this to go over well.

You can do this by starting to clean the dishes and then say something like, "Whoa, whoa, you mean to tell me you didn't like doing dishes this whole time? I've been leaving them for you, thinking you just really enjoyed doing it after a long day of work." This kind of joke has a touch of sarcasm, but there are two important parts that make it inoffensive—the first is the action of actually cleaning, and the second is acknowledging that your guardian has already worked hard all day. If you just said, "What? I thought you liked cleaning" while you're watching television, it would come off as rude and dismissive. The last thing you want is to make anyone feel worse than they already do.

DISCOVER WHAT MAKES YOU LAUGH

The best way to master humor is by paying attention to what makes you laugh. Whenever something makes you laugh, take note of what about it was funny. It's important to remember, though, that not everyone has the same sense of humor, and that's okay! The good news is that when you find people who *do* have the same sense of humor as you, it's easier to bond with them as potential friends. Although already mentioned above, you can explore what you find funny by watching movies, reading joke books, listening to funny podcasts, watching stand-up comedians, and spending time around people you think are funny.

CHAPTER FIVE: UNDERSTANDING FEELINGS

Your emotions can take you on a wild ride sometimes. You might feel like you're on top of the world one day and then hit rock bottom the next. You're not alone! Mood swings are a normal part of being a teenager (and even an adult).

As you go through your teenage years, your body is changing a lot; you might feel a bit self-conscious or just want some alone time to deal with all these changes. Let's face it: Some teens might develop faster or slower than others, making things even more stressful. You might notice that your ability to understand and manage your emotions is evolving as well. This is a natural process that happens as your body and mind go through some major changes. You might find that you're more aware of your own feelings as well as the emotions of those around you. It can be tough to navigate these newfound emotions in the midst of school and other activities, but it's important to learn how to manage them effectively.

For some teens, tackling new challenges and gaining independence can be exciting, while others might feel like they need some extra support to build their confidence. But regardless of where you fall on that spectrum, there are plenty of ways to improve your emotional development. You can learn new skills, identify your unique qualities, and even take steps to strengthen your body and mind.

IT'S OKAY TO HAVE FEELINGS!

Being a teenager can be overwhelming. You and your peers are trying to figure out what you like and who you are, all while taking on more responsibilities and undergoing physical changes. You might want to explore and make your own decisions. All of these factors can trigger emotional responses, and hormonal changes in the body can exaggerate these feelings, making them more overwhelming and harder to control. It's completely normal to feel sad, anxious, or upset, and if you don't know how to manage those feelings, it can lead to unhealthy behaviors.

It's important to embrace your feelings. Instead of trying to push them away, give yourself permission to explore them. The only time emotions are destructive is if they push you to take actions that harm you or others. You can prevent this by first learning to recognize when your emotions are escalating. The moment you start to feel sad or angry, try finding a way to step aside and be alone for a moment. This will give you space to do whatever you need to take care of yourself in private. If you're at school, ask if you can go to the restroom, library, or nurse's office. All these places are quiet, and it's easy to have some time alone to decompress in a healthy way. If you're at home, try doing something physical like going for a walk, cleaning your room, or putting on music to dance to if you're feeling anxious or angry. If you're sad, try a hot bath or shower. The warm water can help soothe you, and the privacy of the tub will give you a great place to cry if needed.

Instead of trying to suppress your emotions, sit back and observe them without judgment. Imagine that they're nothing more than dark clouds passing through your life. Whatever you're feeling, no matter how intense it may seem, it will pass. Paying attention to how you feel and even where you make mistakes will help you have empathy for your peers who are also experiencing similar feelings.

47

As a teenager, you might feel like there are a lot of things in your life that you can't control. This can be scary and frustrating, but it can also free you up to focus on what you can influence if you try. We'll never be able to control another person's actions or certain events in our lives, but when we are frustrated with these things in life, we can help regain a sense of control by focusing on what's in our power. For example, you can't decide how your teacher grades an essay, but you can determine the amount of effort you put into writing the essay. You can't control if your parents will allow you to go to a party, but you can show them you're responsible and trustworthy through your actions.

UNDERSTANDING YOUR PEERS' BODY LANGUAGE AND EMOTIONS

Body language may seem like a complicated topic, but you'll be surprised by how much you already pick up intuitively. Body language is basically how you show your emotions on the outside. It's like a story that your body tells without you even having to say anything.

Now, understanding body language takes some time and practice, but it's definitely worth it. Paying attention to others' physical cues can help you learn how to communicate with people without words. Although there are thousands of subtle signals, some of the most common ones include facial expressions, hand gestures, posture, and eye contact.

When it comes to communicating, did you know that most of what you say doesn't come out of your mouth? The majority of messages in any conversation are revealed through body language. Even though it's such a big part of how we communicate, most people aren't aware of the signals they're sending or how they're being interpreted. That's why learning to read and use body language is so important. It can help you build intimacy, show professionalism, and just generally communicate more effectively.

Think about it: You use your face, hands, posture, and more to talk to your peers, and they're doing the same back to you. It's like a secret code that you and your friends can use to understand each other better.

Before we go over some of the basic forms of body language, it's important to remember that no matter how much you practice, you won't be able to know what someone is thinking for sure unless you ask them. Studying these cues here can help you with communication, but be careful to avoid using them to jump to conclusions or make assumptions. We often learn to mask our body language for various reasons, which is why it shouldn't be treated like a perfect science. Plus, different cultures may have varying interpretations of particular gestures or cues.

Posture can give us a clue about how someone is feeling. If someone is tired, sad, or insecure, they're more likely to slouch, which is when your shoulders curl over your chest. If a person is feeling good and confident, they're more likely to stand up straight.

Eye contact can indicate many things. First, it's important to note that sometimes people aren't comfortable making eye contact in general and it doesn't have a deeper meaning. Other times, maintaining eye contact is a good sign that a person is paying attention, while failing to maintain eye contact could signify boredom, annoyance, distraction, or something else.

Smiling doesn't always mean someone is happy. Many people learn to smile as a way of being polite during a conversation. It isn't necessarily an indication that they're enjoying an activity or an interaction with another person.

Mirroring is when people copy each other's body language without meaning to. This usually happens when people are fully focused on each other. For example, if you prop your head up on your elbow and then the person across from you copies that gesture, it's most likely because they're fully invested in the conversation and are doing it without thinking about it.

Hand signals can help give clues. For example, if someone tucks their hands into their pockets, this can be a sign that they feel uncomfortable. If their thumbs are out of their pockets or hooked in their belt loops, it can be a sign of confidence. Additional hand gestures are often used to emphasize what people are saying.

Pay attention to any blocking movements. If someone closes off their body to another person, this can indicate

50

discomfort or disinterest. Specific movements include someone crossing their legs or literally putting objects in between them and another person. Keep in mind that this doesn't mean they don't like you. It could just mean they're shy or don't like the topic of conversation.

HOW TO HELP YOUR PEERS

As you grow, challenges are bound to increase for you and your peers as you gain additional independence. Don't be surprised if your peers start to look to you for advice or solutions. It's totally normal to feel like you're not sure how to approach the situation or offer help that's effective and respectful. But there are some simple strategies you can use to be a supportive friend and help your peers when they need it most.

Listen

Listening is key when helping your friends. Whenever someone shares personal information with you, it's an important step in your social life. It doesn't matter how small or insignificant it may seem to you—if they're sharing, then they're sharing a part of themselves with you. Creating a safe and supportive environment for your friends to express themselves is crucial. Try not to interrupt or judge what they're feeling. Instead, show that you care by asking open-ended questions. Remember to be patient, observe their body language, ask clarifying questions, and only offer advice when they ask for it.

Show Empathy

When you show empathy, you're letting the other person know that you understand them and care about what they're going through. One way you can do this is by restating what you're hearing. For example, if they tell you about how they failed a math test after studying really hard to pass, you could say, "That must be frustrating and disappointing after how hard you worked." This lets them know that you heard the core message, and it offers them an opportunity to correct you or further express themselves. Another way you can show empathy is by validating their feelings. If your friend is angry with someone but also feels guilty for being angry, you can reassure them that it's okay to be mad.

Offer Practical Help

It is important to clarify whether or not your friends want help before offering it. Sometimes, asking something as simple as "Do you want comfort or advice?" can go a long way with communication. If your friend is looking for help, it's important to do a quick mental assessment before agreeing. Before committing to help someone, you need to make sure you're qualified and that you have the energy to help. Let's look at each of these items a little closer.

Are you qualified? If your friend is struggling with their mental health, the best way you can help them is by encouraging them to seek out professional help. Although you may have a lot of life experience already, it can be really dangerous to give advice about topics like mental health, addiction, or sex. The professionals who handle these matters have studied them extensively for years. With this said, there are a lot of subjects you are qualified to help with. For example, if they are struggling in drama class, maybe you can help them practice their lines. If they don't like how they look in photos, you can help them take a flattering picture.

Is it ethical? If your friend asks you to do something illegal or against your values, you should say no. If what they ask you to do makes you uncomfortable in any way, the answer should be no. There are usually better options that you could suggest instead. For example, if your friend is upset about their test scores and asks to copy your homework, you could refuse but then offer to help them figure out the problems on their own. Having someone show them how to do their homework in a different way than the teacher might be enough for it to click for them.

Do you have the time and energy? Before you can help anyone, you need to take care of yourself first. If you commit to helping someone when you don't have the time or energy, it can create resentment or tensions between the two of you. Furthermore, it can put you in a position where you can't take care of your responsibilities.

EVERYONE IS DIFFERENT

Seeking to understand people will help you socialize with them better. Everyone is different. Some people don't like feeling pressured to speak, and others will overshare when they're nervous. Some people prefer parallel play where they work on individual projects side by side, while others need to have quality time doing things together to feel bonded. The important thing to remember is that there is no right or wrong personality. You can get along with each other better by mutually learning about and communicating your needs.

Although you can look up specific personality types, chances are that few people you meet will know exactly which one they have. The best way to figure out what people need is by asking them directly and setting healthy boundaries with one another. This also means expressing your needs. For example, if you need alone time to feel your best, then you should say so.

Another way you can improve your relationships is by studying the five love languages, which are:

- Words of affirmation
- Quality time
- Physical touch
- Acts of service
- Receiving gifts

When we say love languages, we are not referring to anything necessarily romantic. They are just ways in which people give and receive affection of any kind. So, with your friends, these are important because they can help you comfort those closest to you. Understanding these can really help you take care of your siblings and family as well. When you know your love languages, you can also clearly communicate to your people how to help you on days you feel stressed or sad. Below are some ways to show appreciation to your loved ones based on what makes them feel valued.

Words of affirmation: For these people, giving them compliments or reassurance will let them know you care. This can sometimes include validation as well. Letting them know it wasn't their fault, that it's okay to feel what they are feeling, that everything will be okay, that they did do a good job, or helping hype them up will go a long way.

Quality time: These people need one-on-one time that's meaningful. That means that if you're both on your phones, they probably won't feel satisfied unless you've mutually decided to decompress side by side in that way. Going on a hike, cooking a meal, taking a class, or even playing a board game with these kinds of people will help them feel connected and appreciated.

Physical touch: Some people are comforted by touch. Ways you can express this platonically are in the form of hugs or a consoling touch on the shoulder. It's important that you have consent before touching another person as some people are the exact opposite and feel uncomfortable with being touched.

Acts of service: People whose love language is acts of service will show who they are by going above and beyond for those they love. The problem is that they rarely express when they need help. This can lead to communication issues, especially in households. You can show these types of people you care by doing things for them before they ask. If this is a sibling, helping clean up a shared space is a good way to show this. If it's your guardian, doing the dishes or cooking dinner without being asked might make them happy.

Receiving gifts: Gift giving can be really fun, especially when it's reciprocated. If you have a friend whose love language is gifts, bringing them a coffee or a self-care item will make them feel special. It's important not to give more than you have or to a point that makes you uncomfortable, though, no matter how much you like the person. In a healthy relationship, both people will reciprocate these acts of kindness.

CHAPTER SIX:
IT'S OKAY TO ASK FOR HELP

You might be going through a tough time with your emotions. Sometimes, it feels like nobody gets you—not your parents, not your friends. It can be tough dealing with everything from mood swings to school struggles to figuring out who you are. You might be tempted to keep everything inside and try to handle it on your own. After all, you're growing up, and you want to be independent, right? But here's the thing: You don't have to do it alone. There's no shame in asking for help when you need it.

Here are some of the most common reasons why seeking help is totally worth it:

Depression: If you feel like you're struggling with your mood or experiencing symptoms of depression, it's important to seek professional advice. If left undiagnosed and untreated, these issues can continue into adulthood and interfere with your daily life and relationships with your peers. That's why it's crucial to get help sooner rather than later. Don't wait until things get worse! If you feel irritable, sad, or socially withdrawn, it's time to take action. Reach out to a trusted adult or a health care provider to let them know how you're feeling. They can help you get the proper diagnosis and treatment you need.

Anxiety disorders: Anxiety disorders are pretty common, and it's totally normal to worry about stuff like school, your future, and relationships. But the thing is that anxiety can affect different people in different ways. You might be dealing with severe anxiety or even panic attacks. If left untreated, anxiety and panic disorders can be debilitating. Some common symptoms include feeling nervous or on edge all the time, having trouble sleeping, constantly worrying about things, and struggling with negative thoughts. Talk with a trusted adult if you have concerns about your level of anxiety.

Behavioral issues: You might find yourself going through some behavioral changes such as being aggressive, intentionally rude, or even breaking the rules. Sometimes, our emotions can lead us to form bad habits, which can be both physical and mental. These can range from eating disorders to outbursts to simply being in a pattern of procrastinating on homework. But don't worry;

58

with the right therapy and support, you can understand the root cause of these issues and learn skills to handle each situation.

Addiction and substance abuse: If you or any of your friends are struggling with substance abuse or addiction, it's important that you don't face it alone. One way to get help is by seeing a therapist who specializes in addiction. They can work with you to develop a personalized treatment plan based on your specific situation. Depending on how serious your problem is, the treatment might involve things like individual therapy, detox, or even inpatient treatment.

Stress: While adults have their own set of stressors like financial responsibilities and careers, you might be feeling pressure to perform well academically, make decisions about your future career, and more. It's a lot to handle, but there are ways to manage it. Consider speaking to your parent or caregiver to ask for suggestions or talk with a guidance counselor at school. There are also plenty of online resources to explore self-care techniques such as meditation or going for a jog.

Self-esteem issues: Almost every teenager goes through a phase where they feel unsure about themselves. It's completely normal to have self-confidence, self-esteem, and self-worth issues during your teen years. But, if you don't address these issues, they can negatively affect your academic and social life in the long run. That's why it's important to seek help if you need it.

Trauma: Traumatic experiences can happen to anyone. It could be something like sexual harassment, a near-death experience, or even just witnessing an accident. Whatever form it takes, trauma can have a serious impact on your mental health. It's important to know that it's okay to seek help if you're struggling to cope with trauma. Therapy can be really helpful in teaching you how to be more resilient and deal with any post-traumatic stress you might be experiencing.

Grief: It's tough to deal with loss and grief, but it's a part of life that nobody can avoid. As a teen, you may find coping with these emotions differently from adults. Losing a loved one can be especially difficult when you don't fully understand the impact it has on your life right away. The good news is that there are ways to deal with the pain and sadness. Talking with family members or a grief counselor can help.

Gender and sexual identity: Another common issue teens struggle with is discovering and understanding their gender identity or sexual orientation. Teens struggling with understanding their self-identity might hesitate to talk to a parent, sibling, or friend out of fear of rejection. When you feel this way, the important thing is that you take the time to feel comfortable with your own thoughts. You don't necessarily need to share with others if you don't feel safe, validated, or otherwise secure in taking that step.

A major reason why you may need to seek help in all of these circumstances is that it can give you a fresh perspective on your problems. Sometimes, when we're stuck in a tough situation or dealing with a difficult emotion, it can be hard to see things clearly. But talking things through with someone else can help you gain a new understanding of what's going on and allow you to come up with new strategies for handling it.

SPEAK UP AND BE HONEST

It's common for most people to wait until they're overwhelmed or burned out to ask for help. Although we've already touched on big issues such as mental health and grief, asking for help for the small everyday things is just as important. Whether you're talking about your responsibilities at home, an issue with a friend at school, or balancing your social life with your homework, most people are willing to help where they can.

Many people feel resistance to asking for help for many reasons. It's truly its own unique form of social skill. It's a common belief that we need to suffer in some form to deserve things, and that's just not always true. Yes, commitment and perseverance toward a goal can sometimes come with discomfort, but there's no glory in undergoing unnecessary stress in our everyday lives. With healthy boundaries and respect for others, there's absolutely nothing wrong with seeking and receiving help for all kinds of small things.

Although not all people can rely on their family unit at home, this can be a natural place to start for many people. Letting your siblings or guardians know you're feeling overwhelmed and being honest about where you're struggling can help them empathize with you. For example, let's say you have an important exam coming up in a difficult class and extracurricular activities to consider. Your responsibilities at home might include doing your laundry, keeping your room clean, and taking out the trash. You're stressed out, so your laundry is piling up. You've remembered to take out the trash, but every time you see the dishes and your laundry piling up, it overwhelms you to the point of shutting down. This is where you would ask for help.

When you do, don't expect anyone to do things for you; instead seek compassion and someone to do them with you. For example, you might offer an exchange with a sibling by saying, "Hey, I'm really overwhelmed right now with [insert responsibilities]. Could you maybe help me knock out the dishes and laundry and then I can help you with your chores?" Just having someone work with you will make the work go faster and feel less daunting. By letting your guardians and family know what's happening, you might be surprised — they may offer more help than expected. If you don't have this level of support at home, you can create the same offer with a friend. It might even be easier to clean someone else's room than it is to clean your own.

People will often be oblivious to your true stress level. This is normal. Your parents, friends, and teachers aren't

62

mind readers, and if you don't let them know what's going on with you, they won't know. This is why it's really important to speak up about what's honestly going on with you. It's true that sometimes people may diminish your struggles. This is a big reason that a lot of people don't speak up. However, it's important to remember that for every person who responds this way, there's one who will validate and help you. You don't have to be honest with everyone. If you don't feel comfortable talking to your guardian, then you can maybe say something to your favorite teacher. For example, you might take a moment after class to say "Hey, I'm a little nervous about [assignment]. I'm trying my best with this class, but I have [responsibilities] on my plate right now, and I'm overwhelmed. If you have any advice, please let me know." They might not have answers for you, but now they know what you're dealing with outside the classroom. You might be surprised at how much this will create a positive ripple effect. They might have time to help you sort out your schedule. They may offer personal tutoring. They might be a little more lenient with your deadlines for the assignment. They may even tell other teachers what's going on if one of the other teachers has a way to help. You never know what's possible until you speak up.

When the people closest to you know what's going on with you, they'll usually find little ways to help. Your friend might not want to help you clean your room, but they'll be more understanding about why you can't hang out that weekend. Just make sure to reciprocate that compassion. By nurturing your friendships, you can strengthen your shared support system. People are more likely to help and give when they know that the same energy will be returned.

In general, it's a good habit to treat those closest to you the way you want to be treated. If your friend comes to you and says they're struggling and need help, think about what you would need in that situation and ask them if they would like help in that form. You can also think about their love language and what makes them feel valued. If your friend is an acts of service kind of person, they'll sincerely appreciate having someone help them with their chores. If they are a gift person, giving them something small when they aren't feeling well can really help lift their mood enough to carry on.

Remember, though, that people can't help unless they know you need it. Even if you outwardly display your emotions, most people will think you want to keep your struggles private if you don't openly and directly share. They're more likely to pretend they don't notice you're worn down – not because they don't care but because they assume that you'll share details when you're ready. Just think about a time when you saw someone that you suspected of going through a hard time, but you didn't want to push them or make them uncomfortable. It's common, and you can make things a lot easier by just letting people know what's happening in your life.

ALLOWING OTHERS TO HELP

You might feel nervous or worried when you need to ask for help; you might worry about being rejected or feel like you're being a burden on others. But here's the thing: It takes a lot of courage to admit that you need assistance, and it's a great way to learn and grow as a person. In fact, there are tons of benefits to asking for help that make it totally worth it!

Why should you be open to receiving help?

It keeps you safe and healthy. Taking care of yourself is important, and asking for support can prevent burnout and keep your mind and body as healthy as possible.

It makes you stronger. Asking for help can be scary if you're worried about being rejected or embarrassed. But hearing "no" is a part of life, and learning to handle it with grace makes you more resilient.

It connects you with others. Humans are social creatures, and asking for help allows you to build connections with others. When you ask for advice or support, you're telling others that you value their opinions and expertise. Plus, it can be a great way to make new friends!

It can make you more productive. Sometimes, you need a fresh perspective on a problem to come up with new ideas and approaches.

It shows that you're a high achiever. Did you know that people who are really good at what they do are often the ones who ask for help the most? They know that getting help is a sign of strength, not a weakness, and that there's always more to learn.

It makes everyone happier. When you ask for help, you're giving others a chance to share their knowledge and expertise. That can make them feel good and enable you to build positive relationships. Plus, getting help can reduce stress and make you feel good too!

It creates a positive culture. When you ask for help and support, you're normalizing the idea that everyone needs help sometimes. That makes it easier for others to ask for assistance and can create a culture of connection and support.

SHOWING APPRECIATION EVEN IF OTHERS CAN'T SOLVE YOUR PROBLEM

Getting help from others is sometimes necessary, and it's essential to show your appreciation for the help you receive.

Saying thank you or writing a note of gratitude can go a long way in strengthening your relationships and creating a sense of community. When people know that you appreciate their help, they'll be more likely to help you again in the future.

It's important to remember that you should always express gratitude for any offer of support that you accept, whether it ends up being useful or not. The goal here is to show your appreciation, not to come across as someone who doesn't acknowledge support.

Receiving help from others is a great way to learn new things and gain new perspectives. It can also help you build stronger relationships with those around you. It's a simple but effective way to show that you appreciate and value the people in your life who are there to support you.

How to Show Gratitude

First, it's crucial to recognize that a person meant well and tried to help you. Even if their efforts weren't successful in solving your problem, let them know how much you appreciate their willingness to lend a hand. Acknowledging their assistance will show that you value their support.

When expressing gratitude, be precise and specific about what you're thankful for. Highlight the specific actions or efforts made by the person to assist you, and explain how those efforts were beneficial.

Focus on the positive aspects of the experience, even if the person wasn't successful in helping you. Try to discuss what you took away from the experience or how it enabled you gain a fresh perspective on the situation. By doing this, you're showing that you're able to find the

67

good in any situation and that you appreciate the attempt to help.

Empathy is important too. Put yourself in the other person's shoes and try to understand why they might not have been able to help you effectively. Maybe they were dealing with personal challenges or difficulties, which made it harder for them to provide the assistance you needed.

Remember that receiving help is not just about getting the right solution; it's about valuing the effort and intent behind it.

CHAPTER SEVEN: IT'S OKAY TO SAY NO

Saying no can be tough, especially as a teenager. Sometimes, you might feel like you have to say yes to everything in order to please others or avoid conflict. But the truth is that saying no is your right, and it isn't automatically a bad thing to do. Sure, it might feel uncomfortable at first. You might worry that you're letting someone down or that you're being selfish. But saying no doesn't mean you're a bad person or that you don't care about others. It just means that you're prioritizing your own needs and boundaries, which is important. Think about the times when you've said yes to something and then regretted it later. Maybe you ended up feeling resentful or burned out. That's not good for anyone.

That's why it's important to permit yourself to say no when it's truly necessary. It's not about being selfish or rude—it's about taking care of yourself and being honest with others. And who knows? Saying no might actually lead to a better outcome for everyone involved. For example, if a friend asks you to do something that you know will be too much for you, saying no might help them find someone who can do it better, or it might help them realize that they need to ask for help in a different way.

Get used to saying no to requests from others and become more confident in your ability to do so. Never forget that you have the freedom to choose how you utilize your time. Remember that you always have the freedom to decline an offer. It doesn't imply that you're engaging in some kind of unchangeable, selfish action. It indicates that you're saying no because the request conflicts with your schedule or moral principles, and that's okay.

WHAT TO DO WHEN SOMEONE TELLS YOU NO

Don't Take Things Personally

Throughout your lifetime, you'll run into situations where people have to turn you down. When this happens, it rarely means anything deeper than that. It's not a reflection on you as a person or an intentional slight.

If you don't get the help or support you were hoping for, don't hold a grudge or see the person as your enemy. Everyone has their own requests and needs, and you won't always be able to fulfill them all. That's just the way life works.

Remember that others have their own things going on too, and it's important for them to honor their boundaries in order to keep showing up in the relationship with a positive mindset.

Be Curious

Try your best to avoid getting frustrated when someone tells you no without explaining why. Sometimes people forget to give their reasoning, or maybe they're just in a hurry. Other people may feel uncomfortable explaining themselves because they've had bad experiences in the past with people trying to use that information to change their minds. By asking politely and respectfully, you might gain a better understanding of the situation. It's important, though, to avoid using this information to try to manipulate the outcome. If someone says no, respect it and don't try to push them to do something they don't want to do. After all, you'll want that same respect returned when it comes to protecting your time and boundaries.

Listen and Understand

When someone says no to you, listening to what they're saying and trying to understand their perspective can help you see their side. By doing so, you can avoid making assumptions or jumping to conclusions. You'll also gain a better understanding of the situation, which can allow you to come up with a plan for moving forward. Instead of assuming the worst or getting upset, take a step back and put yourself in their shoes. Try to see things from their point of view. By doing this, you'll gain insight into their decision-making process, and you might even discover a new way of approaching the situation.

Find Alternatives

It doesn't mean it's the end of the road just because someone turns down your request. There are still plenty of other options available to you. Take a moment to brainstorm some alternative solutions or approaches. This can help you find a compromise or a different way of achieving your goal. It's a good idea to center yourself and consider what's within your control. You might need the help of another person or you could suggest a compromise. For example, maybe your friend can't help you with something but your sibling can. Maybe your guardian says no to you going out on the weekend, but they say yes to you having friends over instead.

Don't Give Up Yet

If you've recently been disappointed, don't give up just yet. It can be tough, but there are ways to get help. Sometimes, it's all about finding the right approach. If someone tells you no, respect their decision, but don't give up on what you're pursuing. Instead, try a different strategy, maybe with a different person. Persistence and determination are key to achieving your goals, but when dealing with other people's boundaries, you need to be careful to maintain a healthy mindset.

Here's an example: There's a tire swing that goes out over a ledge and into the water below. You know it's safe because your guardian tested it, but your friend is still terrified of going and says no every time you ask. You don't want to go alone, though. So, what can you do? Instead of giving up on trying out the tire swing, find solutions that respect your friend's boundaries and give you what you want. Ask them if they'll hang out nearby while you go, and make sure that they know you'll respect their boundary of not wanting to participate. Another option is to see if other people want to go along with you. Just because that one particular friend isn't interested doesn't mean no one else will be.

Take Responsibility for What Happens Next

If you don't get something done because you didn't get help, you're still going to be the one who has to face the consequences. It's important to take responsibility for your own actions and behavior instead of focusing your energy on what other people did. Don't blame others or make excuses. Instead, focus on what you can do to improve the situation or achieve your goal. At the end of the day, success is all about taking action and making things happen.

Learn From It

If someone turns you down, take a step back and reflect on how you made your request before. Were you in a rush? Did you come across as entitled or impolite? Did you ask for too much? It's important to see if there's anything you could have done better. When someone says no, it can actually be a chance to learn and improve. Use this opportunity to reflect on what happened and see what you can learn from it. This way, you can avoid making the same mistake in the future when you try again.

Accept the Situation and Move On

Sometimes, situations are just out of your hands. In these moments, it's best to take a moment to yourself before reacting. If possible, get a good night's sleep in before doing anything else. It's okay to be upset, sad, disappointed, or frustrated. It is not okay to try to force someone to do what you want.

It's okay to be excited or hopeful, but remaining realistic and accepting situations as they are is really important. Just because one person said no doesn't mean that the right person will, and now you have a clearer of idea of what you're looking for in the future. This goes for all things. Maybe you didn't get a part in a play or someone wasn't interested when you asked them out on a date. By considering what you hoped would happen versus what actually happened, you might gain insight on what you need to work on for next time.

Maintain a Positive Attitude

Disappointment is hard. There's no way around it, though. Keeping a positive outlook can be difficult, but there are a few things that can help. If you're disappointed, refocus on what you are grateful for in the situation. Start with the smallest, silliest items and then build up from there. You can also take a moment to remember that there's a lesson in most situations. By finding the lesson, you can assign meaning to the moment, which can help with accepting it. And it's okay to not be okay. You can accept the situation and still feel sad about it. In that case, remember that the feelings will pass. It's just a bad moment or an excuse to indulge in some self-care.

75

WAYS TO SAY NO WITHOUT ACTUALLY SAYING THE WORD

So far in this chapter, we've been talking about some tough truths, but now let's shift gears and talk about different ways you can say no to other people. Sometimes, people will come to you asking for help, and it can be hard to refuse without offending them or coming across as rude. But there will be times when you just have to decline a request. Luckily, there are many ways to say no without actually using the word itself.

When someone asks you for help or a favor, it's important to think about whether or not you're able to help them. If you can't, it's okay to decline politely. Here are some alternative ways to say no that might work for you:

"I'm super busy right now"

When someone asks you to do something and you have too much on your plate already, you can use this phrase. Although you don't owe anyone an explanation, you can give the person a little insight into what your schedule looks like if you want them to understand. You don't have to do this, though. It's no one else's business to know what you're busy with, and you can be busy taking care of yourself, even if this just entails something simple like playing with your pet. If you don't have the time or energy for it, then it's okay to decline.

"I'm not sure I can do that at this time"

Instead of flat out rejecting the request, you can simply say that you're not sure you can commit at this time. For example, maybe someone is pushing you to join a sports team or take on a long-term project. Rather than saying no, you can say something like, "I'm not sure I can do that at this time, but thanks for considering me." This way, you're being honest about your availability and not committing to something you're not sure you can handle. Remember that it's important to prioritize your own well-being and not take on more than you can handle. When using this phrase, though, it's polite to commit to a time when you'll know for sure. For example, if someone invites you to a birthday party, you might say, "I'm not sure I can go, but I can let you know by Friday." Sometimes, delaying giving an answer by one day is enough time for you to really think on what the right course of action is for you.

"I'm grateful for the opportunity, but I can't"

If someone asks you to do something that you really don't want to do, you can be grateful for the opportunity and still decline their request in a single message. For example, you could say, "I appreciate the offer, but I'm going to have to decline this time." This lets the person know that you're not able to help them without being impolite or hurtful. It's important to be honest with people and not agree to something you really don't want to do. You can still be kind and courteous when saying no and let them know that you appreciate their request.

"I'd rather not, but thanks for asking"

"I'd rather not, but thanks for asking" is a polite and respectful way to decline someone's request when you're not interested in doing what they're asking. You can still acknowledge the other person's effort and thoughtfulness in reaching out to you even if you can't fulfill their request. It's a tactful way to communicate your lack of interest without offending or hurting the other person's feelings. So, if you find yourself in a situation where you need to say no, consider using this phrase to decline the request in a respectful manner.

"I'm not a big fan of that sort of stuff"

Instead of just saying no, be honest and say that it's not really your thing. For example, if someone wants you to watch a movie that you're not interested in, you could say something like, "Thanks for asking, but I'm not really into that type of movie." Or, if someone wants you to take up a new hobby that doesn't appeal to you, you could say, "I appreciate the suggestion, but I don't think that's something I would enjoy." If you'd like to do something else with that person, this is a good time to suggest it. "I don't really like eating out, but you're welcome to come to my house for dinner if you want" or "I don't feel

78

comfortable swimming in open water, but I'll go to the pool with you." This can be helpful if you're not trying to reject this person entirely — you just don't want to do that one particular thing. You don't need to tack this on if you're trying to shut something down completely in a kind way.

"I don't feel up to it"

Maybe someone's asking you to hang out or do something that requires energy when you're feeling tired or drained. Instead of saying no, which might seem rude or dismissive, just let them know that you're not feeling up to it. It's a great way to turn down an invitation without offending the other person. For example, you could say, "I appreciate the invite, but I'm not feeling great" or "I'm feeling pretty drained right now. Maybe another time?" However, if you have no intention of hanging out at another time, then it's important to avoid giving false hope.

"That doesn't seem like a good idea"

When someone suggests something that you don't agree with or that you think is a bad idea, it's important to speak up and voice your opinion. You could say, "That doesn't seem like a good idea" as a polite way to disagree. It's important to remember that voicing your opinion can start a conversation and potentially lead to finding a better solution. When you disagree with someone, try to explain your reasoning and offer suggestions for alternatives. This can help the other person understand your perspective and open up the conversation for other ideas and potential remedies.

CHAPTER EIGHT: WHERE CAN YOU BE SOCIAL?

Are you looking for cool places to hang out and meet new people? Nowadays, with social media and technology taking over, it can take time to find spots where you can socialize face to face. But don't worry; there are plenty of fantastic places for you to connect with your peers in real life. Let's check out some of the locations where you can be social and have a good time.

School clubs and activities: First off, school clubs and activities are an excellent place to start. Joining a club or team based on your interests can help you connect with like-minded people. Whether it's sports, music, theater, or debate, participating in extracurricular activities can lead to lasting friendships.

Volunteering: Volunteering is another way to socialize while giving back to the community. Animal shelters, food banks, and nursing homes are just some of the organizations that welcome teen volunteers. Volunteering not only helps you make new friends, but it also fosters a sense of purpose and can expose you to potential mentorships as well.

Local community centers: Local community centers often offer activities and programs specifically designed for teens. There are many opportunities to try new things and meet new people, ranging from sports leagues to art classes. Plus, many community centers offer low-cost or even free programs, making them accessible to teens from all backgrounds. You can usually find these by looking on your city or town website. In addition to this, your city will most likely have a community calendar with events listed.

Youth groups: Whether religious or secular, youth groups provide a sense of belonging and community among peers who share similar values and beliefs. In addition to regular meetings, many youth organizations host fun activities and events like game nights and movie screenings, allowing you to socialize and have fun.

Part-time jobs: Part-time jobs are another great way to meet new people and develop your social skills. Retail, food service, and other customer-facing industries

82

provide plenty of opportunities for social interaction with customers and coworkers. Plus, earning some extra cash can help you gain independence and learn responsibility.

Sports league: Joining a sports league is a fun way to stay active and a great opportunity to connect with new people. Playing soccer, basketball, or any sport as part of a team can help you develop teamwork and build camaraderie. Even if you're not athletic, many sports leagues offer noncompetitive options for beginners.

Summer camps: Lastly, summer camps are a unique opportunity to socialize and have fun while trying new things. There's something for everyone at traditional summer camps, including activities like swimming, hiking, arts and crafts, or science. Plus, you'll meet people from all over the country and even the world, with many camps offering special programs just for that purpose.

KEEPING SAFE WHILE SOCIALIZING

It's amazing how you can now connect with other teens from all over the world thanks to social media and online platforms. But with this comes a whole new set of safety concerns that previous generations didn't have to deal with, which means your parents or caregivers might be completely unaware of some of the safety concerns you'll face in the world today. This is why it's important to do your own research in addition to whatever rules your family already has in place.

Remember that safety should always come first, whether you're online or in a physical location. Safety precautions don't stop when you turn 18. You'll need to learn how to keep yourself safe in adulthood without the protection of your guardians, so it's a good idea to start taking it seriously now. Here are some steadfast tips to keep you and your friends safe:

Share your location: It's a good idea to share your location with at least two people. This doesn't need to be your parent, but it should be people who will actively check up on you to make sure you're okay. This could include a best friend or a sibling.

Let people know your plans: Even if you're just going down the street or hanging out in your neighborhood, it's a good idea to let two people know what your plans are and how to find you if your location disappears or something happens to your phone.

Take a buddy: Whenever possible, take a friend or sibling. Make sure to discuss situations beforehand so that both of you know what you're okay with doing and not doing. For example, if you want to go to a party, make sure your friend is okay with that before roping them in. In another situation, maybe you and your friends have plans to go to a concert together—you should discuss what time you want to leave and what to do if you get separated. Most importantly, go with someone you trust to watch your back.

84

Don't trust strangers: It doesn't matter how nice someone is — don't trust strangers with your personal information or belongings. Don't be alone with them or accept food or drinks from them. If you meet someone your age and you think they could become a friend, you can contact them on social media or ask them to meet up at a public place like a restaurant or a coffee shop.

Keep your private life offline: Social media is a great tool, but it can also be dangerous. Even if you know every single person on your account, people can still find out information that you don't want them to. That's why it's important to keep everything set to private and avoid adding too many personal details such as your email or location.

Be wary of random adds: If someone you don't know randomly adds you on social media, it's a good idea to ignore it. Unfortunately, it's easy to pretend to be something you're not when you're online, and there are many scam artists trying to lure people into all kinds of situations using flattery and false promises. It's really important not to entertain any of these people, and in most cases, reporting them is the best thing you can do to protect others from harm as well.

Take and send photographs to your friends: This may seem a little silly, but if you meet someone new, take a picture together and then send it to a friend or family member with their name. That way, if anything did happen to you, there's a record of who you were with and what they look like. You can also take photos of where you are, license plate numbers, and anything else you feel

85

like photographing to increase your safety. Hopefully, these will only be proof of great memories and nothing more.

Order your own drinks: Even if you are just ordering a glass of water, get it yourself and practice covering the top of the drink with your hand whenever you look away. The idea is to have this become second nature so that you don't even think about it whenever you look away from your drink. You should also watch out for your friends and make sure their drinks are protected too.

WAYS TO BE SOCIAL AT SCHOOL

School is often a central part of your life. It includes teens from different backgrounds and cultures, and navigating the social part of it can be quite demanding. However, school offers numerous chances for you to interact with your peers and be social. Even if you're homeschooled, you can still participate in some of these options or the community equivalent.

Join a club or activity: One of the best ways to be social at school is to join a club or activity. There are tons of options, including sports, music, theater, and debate. By joining a group or activity that interests you, you'll have the chance to meet new people who share your passions. If you're homeschooled, you can find these opportunities through your local performing arts center or designated programs that allow for homeschooled students to participate in public school sports.

Attend school events: School events such as dances, concerts, and sporting events are also great places to meet new people. You can show your school spirit, enjoy live performances, and strike up conversations with classmates in a relaxed setting. If you're homeschooled, you can still attend public school games. This is a great way to meet people supporting both teams. You can usually find these schedules online or by calling the school.

Participate in class discussions: Participating in class discussions is a great way to make friends and learn from your peers. Sharing your ideas and thoughts with others can help you see things from different perspectives and build connections with classmates.

Form a study group: Forming a study group is another way to be social at school. Collaborating with classmates for projects and test preparation can help you learn from each other and develop new relationships. You can still do this if you're homeschooled, but you might need to connect with other students over social media or through neighborhood apps.

Eat lunch with friends: Eating lunch with friends is a simple but effective way to socialize at school. Whether you bring your lunch from home or get it from the school cafeteria, eating with classmates gives you a chance to catch up and strengthen your relationships.

It is important to push yourself outside of your comfort zone and be open to new experiences and individuals. By following these tips, you'll be well on your way to being more social at school and making the most of your school experience!

SOCIAL MEDIA GROUPS AND PLATFORMS

Social media has changed the way people converse and interact with one another. It's become an indispensable part of people's lives, allowing them to interact with others from all over the world who share similar interests and passions.

Use the search functionality: Social media platforms like Facebook, Instagram, Twitter, and Reddit have a search bar that allows you to look for groups and pages related to your interests. For example, if you're into cooking, you can search for cooking groups or recipes. If you love sports, you can search for groups dedicated to your favorite sports team or athlete.

Join recommended groups: Ask your friends or family members to recommend groups or pages that they think you might enjoy. This way, you'll gain access to groups that you might not have discovered otherwise.

Browse popular platforms: Check out popular social media platforms such as Facebook, Instagram, Twitter, and Reddit to find new interests. These platforms have millions of users and offer groups and pages for almost every hobby and interest.

Use hashtags: Hashtags are an excellent way to find relevant content on social media. Use hashtags to search for posts, pages, or groups related to your interests. For example, if you're into fitness, search for hashtags like #fitness or #workout on Instagram or Twitter.

Join niche platforms: There are several niche social media platforms that cater to specific interests and hobbies. Ravelry, for instance, is a social media platform for knitters and crocheters, and Goodreads is a platform for book enthusiasts. Joining these niche platforms will allow you to interact with people who share your interests and passions.

Attend social media events: Meetups, conferences, and workshops on social media are great ways to connect with like-minded people and learn about new organizations and platforms.

Use social media analytics tools: Social media analytics tools can help you identify groups and pages related to particular topics or interests. For example, tools like BuzzSumo can assist you in locating popular social media pages and groups linked to your interests.

Join Facebook groups: Joining Facebook groups is an excellent way to connect with people who share your interests. You can engage in discussions, exchange content, and receive guidance and support from other members.

WAYS TO BE SOCIAL AT HOME

Many individuals prefer to be within their own walls rather than basking in the bustling atmosphere of the street. There are numerous ways to make the most of your time at home. One of the best ways to accomplish this is to create a cozy and comfortable hangout space in your home. You can also plan enjoyable activities for friends and family to participate in. Here are some suggestions for home hangouts to get you started:

Host a game night: Get your friends or family together for a classic game night. Choose from board games, card games, or video games, and make it even more special by preparing some snacks and drinks to share. You can even set up a recurring event by changing who hosts the game each time.

Have a movie marathon: Take it easy with a movie night. Choose a theme or genre, pick a few films to watch back to back, make some popcorn, and settle in for a relaxing evening on the sofa. You can even turn your living room into a home theater experience by setting up a projector and screen.

Plan a DIY project: Get your creative juices flowing by planning a do-it-yourself project with friends or family. Choose something easy like painting or crafting, or take on a bigger challenge such as building furniture or redecorating a room. Not only will you have fun bonding with your loved ones, but you'll also have a tangible result at the end.

Cook a meal together: Cooking is a fun and rewarding hobby to share with friends or family. Choose a recipe that everyone will enjoy and prepare the meal together. You'll get the chance to work on your social skills while you collaborate on the meal and you can continue your conversation as you eat a delicious meal after. You could even make it a regular thing by taking turns and hosting dinner parties.

Host a book club: Start a book group with your friends if you love reading. Each month, choose a book to read and then get together to discuss your thoughts and opinions. You could even take it up a notch and throw a book-themed party with a competition and a prize.

Have a spa day: Take a break and pamper yourself with a spa day at home with friends or family. Do some face masks, give each other manicures, or simply relax with some aromatherapy. Set the mood with some calming music and dim lighting.

Plan a virtual hangout: When meeting in person isn't possible, organize a virtual game night, a Netflix party, or even a virtual workout using video conferencing tools such as Zoom and Google Meet to stay connected with friends and family.

Host a themed party: Who says you need a reason to throw a party? Choose a theme like a decade or a color scheme and invite your friends over for a fun evening.

91

Make it a potluck and ask everyone to bring a dish that matches the theme.

CHAPTER NINE: BALANCING RESPONSIBLITIES AND ENTERTAINMENT

Part of having a healthy social life is finding balance between your friends and your responsibilities. If you give too much energy to either one, it can leave you feeling drained and ungrounded. Right now, you may have guardians, teachers, and coaches helping you maintain balance by giving you curfews and study blocks or grounding you if your grades drop. However, once you're an adult, you'll have to manage these things on your own. It's a good idea to practice self-regulating now so that the transition is easier.

One way you can tell if you're out of balance is if you feel like you're reacting to your environment more than intentionally designing it. If you feel like you don't have enough time or space to get everything you need done, it can leave you feeling stressed and unfocused. In these moments, the best thing you can do for yourself is to take a time out and refocus. You can do this by looking at what needs done versus what you want to do. Dedicate your attention to the most important things and then take a break to care for your body and reorganize your thoughts and priorities.

Ideally, your schedule should have a healthy balance. You should have small pockets of social time dispersed throughout your day and the occasional full day to relax and enjoy your hobbies and friends. You also need enough time for chores, hygiene, family, and studying. Finding what works best for you will take trial and error.

When you work on your schedule, pay attention to what leaves you feeling good or bad and when you naturally deviate from your plan. What works best for you might not work for someone else. Some people function best by spending 15 to 30 minutes a day on their chores, while other people prefer to deep clean once a week and only complete short daily tasks like cleaning up their desk or washing the dishes. The same thing goes for homework. You don't want to procrastinate on your schoolwork until right before your deadline, but some people need to complete their homework in short bursts.

Once you find out what style works best for you, you can start tweaking your routine. Sometimes, adding in small elements like the right kind of snacks, your favorite music, or even a partner working independently next to you can make these moments a lot more fun and fulfilling in the long run.

TIME MANAGEMENT

The first step to managing your time effectively is understanding that you have the same 24 hours in a day to do the things you love and the things that will build a better future.

When planning, prioritizing, and organizing your tasks, it's a good idea to start with the basic, unmovable building blocks first. Block off 10 hours for sleep, even if you don't sleep the whole time. This gives you a little time to get things ready for the morning and do a quiet activity away from electronics like reading a book, journaling, or completing an art project before falling asleep.

You also need time for daily exercise and hygiene. Even if you don't complete a workout plan or go on long runs, you can still take 30 minutes to do something active. Whether it's walking your dog, gardening, playing in the snow, or going on a bike ride, this is a small habit that will help keep you feeling good even when you have a lot on your plate. Hygiene routines are an act of self-care and will look different for each person. Washing your face, brushing your teeth, shaving, and taking a shower are pretty basic elements to a hygiene routine. Some people might extend these to include deeper skin care and pampering. This is a good time to really enjoy yourself and take some quiet time. If you enjoy bubble baths, for example, you should add these into your hygiene routine to help you relax before bed.

School is also fixed obligations that you need to do. As you get older, the hours you are expected to go to school or work will change, but as a teenager, the time you need to spend at school should be pretty consistent. Try to enjoy the little pockets of space between classes and on your lunch break as much as possible. You might assign a certain portion of your day for reviewing homework, but if you can do this with a friend, it will make it a more fulfilling experience. Trying to pack too much into your school days could give you more time later, but it's really easy to push yourself too hard and end up feeling completely exhausted by the end of the day.

Social activity can be tricky to balance, especially if you want to spend all your time having fun with friends. On the weekends, though, it's a good idea to make plans ahead. As you get older, people's schedules will become tighter, and it can become hard to keep friendships alive without active planning. Therefore, it's a good idea to start practicing now. Ask your family what they have in mind for the weekend, and then if there's space for it, plan something fun with a buddy.

When planning your schedule, leave extra time in case anything changes. Things outside of your control will happen, and it's good to have a little wiggle room to adjust things as needed.

What Happens When You Mismanage Your Time

Increased stress and anxiety: When you don't manage your time well, you may feel increased stress and anxiety. Going from one task to the next without any breaks can take a toll on your emotional and physical health. You need time to relax and recharge to avoid feeling overwhelmed.

A decline in productivity: Attempting to do too many things at once can actually lead to a decline in productivity. You may start making more mistakes, forgetting important tasks, and struggling to finish your work on time. This can add to your stress levels and create a cycle of anxiety.

Burnout: Pushing yourself too hard for an extended period can result in burnout. Burnout is a condition of physical and emotional exhaustion that can make even the simplest tasks difficult. It can cause depression, despair, and even physical illness.

A neglected social life: If you don't manage your time well, you may end up neglecting your social life. You may not have time to spend with your friends or pursue your hobbies and interests. This can lead to feelings of loneliness and isolation, which can aggravate anxiety and depression.

Focus on Pacing, and Give Yourself Time

A secret to successful time management is pacing yourself and giving yourself enough time to get things done without feeling overwhelmed. Trying to estimate how long a task will take is usually inaccurate. It's better to time how long everything takes so that you have a realistic picture for next time. It's important to time yourself completing the task when you aren't rushing and have plenty of time to do what needs to be done in an easy, relaxed manner. You'll be surprised to find that some tasks take much less time to complete than you thought, while others need more time.

You shouldn't pressure yourself or rush head-on into tasks without thinking them through. Don't hop from one task to another without direction. Instead, use these well-researched tips and strategies for improving your time-management skills:

Prioritize your tasks: Identify the most important tasks or the ones with the shortest deadlines, such as studying for an exam or attending a family function. Once you know your priorities, you can plan your time accordingly.

Use a calendar: It's important to keep track of your schedule and commitments, so use a planner or digital calendar to visualize your schedule and ensure that you don't overlook any essential tasks or activities.

Learn to say no: While being involved in many activities is great, it's important not to overextend yourself. If you're feeling overwhelmed or stressed, consider saying no to extra obligations that may not be necessary.

Avoid multitasking: Studies have shown that multitasking can reduce productivity and increase stress levels. Instead, focus on one task at a time, and give it your full attention to complete it faster and with fewer errors.

Take breaks: It's important to take breaks throughout the day to recharge and avoid burnout. Find ways to relax, such as going for a short walk, listening to music, or doing deep breathing exercises.

Communicate with others: Don't be afraid to seek guidance and support from your parents, teachers, or counselors if you're feeling overwhelmed or struggling to balance your different obligations.

Practice self-care: Getting enough sleep, eating healthy, and exercising regularly will keep you energized and focused throughout the day while reducing your stress levels.

Learn to adapt: Remember that life is unpredictable and things don't always go as planned. It's important to be flexible with changes in your schedule or commitments and not to be too hard on yourself if you need to make adjustments or take a break from certain pursuits.

Celebrate: Take time to celebrate your achievements and successes, no matter how small. Recognize your progress toward achieving a balanced life, and give yourself credit for your hard work and dedication. Balancing all of life's responsibilities as a teenager can be challenging, but it's not impossible.

By using these strategies, you can manage your time effectively, prioritize your tasks, and find a balance between various responsibilities. Remember that finding balance is an ongoing process, so be patient and stay committed to your goals.

Working Together and Sharing Responsibilities

Managing your time isn't just about keeping track of your own responsibilities. It's also helping your friends with their tasks. Believe it or not, pitching in can actually help you improve your own time-management skills. By helping others, you'll learn new ways of handling situations and gain valuable experience that you can apply to your own life.

For instance, maybe your friend needs help organizing their study schedule. By assisting them, you'll learn new techniques for prioritizing tasks and allocating time efficiently. Plus, you'll get the satisfaction of knowing you've helped someone out, which can be a great motivator for staying on top of your own responsibilities. Here are some tips on how to do that while still keeping everything in balance:

Study with friends: Instead of slogging through the material on your own, you can divide and conquer when working as a team. Each of you can take a chapter or a topic, learn it well, and then teach it to the rest of the group. This way, you'll be able to learn from each other and keep each other motivated.

Chore buddies: Chores are another area where teamwork can make a big difference. Instead of feeling bored or overwhelmed, you can team up with a buddy and make it fun! You can chat, listen to music, or even make a game out of it. Plus, when you work together, you'll finish faster and have more time for other activities. And who knows? You might even start to enjoy doing chores!

Volunteer together: Volunteering is a great way to give back to your community while making new friends. You can find opportunities to volunteer at a local charity, school, or religious center. This way, you'll be helping others while feeling good about yourself. Plus, volunteering can be a great way to learn new skills and gain experience.

Honing Your Time-Management Skills

Having good time-management skills is crucial not just for school but also for your future. It will help you become more productive, efficient, and organized in your daily life.

Living a life where everything is already planned out might seem easy, but it won't help you become a pro at managing your time. At some point, your usual schedule will get disrupted and you'll have to adjust your plans. If you're someone who lives a very structured life, you might struggle with adapting to those changes.

To avoid that, you need to learn how to manage your time wisely. You can't just go through your daily routine and expect to magically have excellent time-management skills. It's important to be aware of your schedule and make adjustments when necessary. By doing this, you'll be better equipped to handle unexpected changes and adapt to them quickly. Here are some steps that you can take to improve your time-management skills:

Develop routines: First up, it's important to establish routines. By practicing healthy habits like doing your chores right after school, taking breaks when needed, and getting enough sleep, you'll be able to stay on track and avoid wasting time. Turning your plans into routines will help you know exactly what to do at every turn, leaving you with more time to do the things you love.

Use tools: Another useful tip is to make use of time-management tools. There are plenty of apps and software programs out there that can help you plan and organize your day. Tools like Time Doctor, Calendar, Trello, Evernote, and Momentum Dash can help you prioritize your tasks, work faster, and avoid distractions. If you can't download apps, you can either make or purchase a planners. You can even just create lists that are curated specifically to your needs. A really easy way to create a reusable checklist for routines is by using a dry erase marker and a page protector sheet with your list inside. You can wipe the slate clean every day and change the lists as needed. By using these tools, you'll be able to see how your time is being spent and make adjustments.

Control your use of the internet: Electronic gadgets can be huge time-wasters. While they're useful for staying connected with friends and family and keeping up with the latest news, they can also be a major source of distraction. To avoid falling down the social media rabbit hole, set limits on the amount of time you spend on your phone or computer. You might also want to try a digital detox by taking a break from your devices altogether. By taking control of your use of electronic gadgets and social media, you'll be able to focus on the things that really matter.

If you see a peer who seems organized and is able to handle all of their school work and extracurriculars easily, they might be a good person to ask for advice. Family and teachers can also help you, and there are many free videos available online with different techniques to manage your time. Everyone works differently, so hearing many different perspectives can help guide you. You can develop habits and routines now, then continue to tweak them throughout your life to help you live in a happy, healthy, and balanced way.

Honing your time management skills takes practice, so don't worry if it takes some time to get the hang of it. Remember to take breaks, stay focused, and use your time effectively. Before long, you'll be well on your way to managing your time like a pro!

CHAPTER TEN: HOW TO HANDLE MONEY

Managing money is an essential skill, and your teenage years are an optimal time to learn it. Whether it's money you've earned from a part-time job, an allowance, or gifts from family and friends, there are many things you can do with it to practice being financially responsible.

Knowing how to handle your money will come in handy as you develop your social skills and start spending money out with friends. It can be tempting to splurge when you're out with a group, especially if you're celebrating a special occasion like someone's birthday.

But even though it might not be fun to think about how much you have to spend, the last thing you want is to spoil your evening by realizing you went overboard.

Educating yourself on finances is the first step to making the most of your money and picking the right activities to do while socializing. Personal finance topics such as budgeting, saving, and investing can help you make wise financial decisions now and in the future. Luckily, many resources are available to help you learn about these topics. You can find books, podcasts, and online courses that cover personal finance. Your school may also offer classes or workshops on financial literacy. Take advantage of these resources to learn as much as you can.

Investing your money wisely is also critical to building wealth. While investing can be intimidating, it doesn't hurt to learn about different strategies at a young age. One option is to open a savings account or a certificate of deposit (CD). These are low-risk investment options that offer a guaranteed return on your investment. Another option is to invest in stocks or mutual funds. While these investments come with more risk, they can offer higher returns over the long term. Many of these investments are only available once you've over the age of 18, but your parents or guardians may be able to assist you by setting up a joint account.

Another crucial aspect of managing your money is budgeting. If you receive a set amount of money each month from your parents or your job, it's essential to plan how you'll spend it. Make a budget that outlines your expenses and income, and make sure to stick to it. By

106

budgeting, you can avoid overspending and ensure that you have enough money for the things you need.

Pay off any expenses you might have first. These might include contributions to your family, car insurance, gas, a phone bill, snacks, or upcoming extracurricular fees. Usually, these numbers are the same every month. For expenses like gas and snacks that vary, it's a good idea to record how much you're spending. You can do this by keeping a little notebook in your car and writing down the numbers or you can save your receipts somewhere like a sandwich bag in your glove compartment. When you have a few months or even weeks of purchases, you can put your math skills to the test and find out how much you're spending on average per week. It's a good idea to add a little extra to this number to give you some wiggle room. The rest of your income can then be divided between savings and spending.

Consider setting aside a portion of your monthly income into a savings account. You can talk to your parents or your bank for more details. In general, 10 percent of your income should go into an interest-building savings account.

Saving money is important. It takes lots of time to save up for things without stress. In the future, you're likely to acquire things like a car, apartment, or house that will need constant maintenance; when something breaks down, it will often happen randomly. Without a savings account, this is extremely stressful and inconvenient. Ideally, you should aim to have three times your monthly income in your savings account as your first goal.

Whenever you have to spend from this fund or your income increases, it's a good habit to return to this foundational goal.

When considering what your savings goals are, think about what kind of life you want to live. If you want to travel, buy a cute home, study abroad, get a nice car, or revamp your wardrobe, you'll need to save additional money outside of your emergency fund. Even stashing little bits away will help dramatically. If you earn tips, many people will either choose to save all their tips as a rule or only use their tip money to pay for certain expenses. Make saving a priority, and you'll be surprised at how quickly your savings can grow.

Right now, your bills and expenses are probably lower than at any other time in your life, and it may seem tempting to spend what you have available. However, having fewer bills creates a great opportunity to build the life you want through smart spending practices. Ideally, you should spend less than 20 percent of your income on things you want, which includes socializing and developing your social skills through activities that cost money.

When planning your spending budget, think about the things you truly enjoy. If you like to get coffee occasionally or see a movie, it's a good idea to set aside money for that. If going to concerts is something you enjoy, plan ahead and stash this money aside. Get used to getting rid of small expenditures to make room to pay for really good experiences. This might mean only getting fancy coffees when you're out with a friend or only

108

buying clothes that you really like. Having a list of what you actually want to spend your money on (e.g., road trips with friends, concerts, coffee dates, or movies) will help you decide if a purchase is worth it.

When you go to buy yourself something, ask if you really need it or if buying it will take away from being able to do the things on your list in the future. For example, let's say you just got paid and you have money. Stop and think first. Even if you don't have plans yet, something could come up. Making a frivolous purchase could take away a valuable experience between that moment and your next paycheck. For all you know, your favorite band could announce that they're coming to town and ticket prices are affordable if bought immediately. Your crush might ask you out to the movies, or your best friend might call you up for a spontaneous road trip where you'll want to splurge a little.

Although money will never buy you true friendship, it can be a great tool for building memories. Even if you only have a little bit, saving that money you would spend buying snacks for yourself alone could instead be spent on purchasing snacks to share at a sleepover or doing something fun with a friend. It's best to have enough set aside for possible experiences than to waste your money on things that will only increase your quality of life a little bit.

MONEY CAN BE USED FOR GIFTS

Giving gifts is an excellent way to show appreciation. When you give gifts to your friends, you're not only showing them how much you care, but you're also strengthening your bond with them. Although some people may argue that gift-giving isn't necessary in friendships, there are several reasons why it's essential and worthwhile to do so.

When you give a gift to someone, it shows that you care about them and are thinking of them even when they're not around. This can be especially important in long-distance friendships where physical distance can make staying connected difficult. A thoughtful gift can serve as a physical reminder of your relationship and keep it strong.

Another reason why giving gifts to friends is important is that it can be a way to commemorate special occasions or milestones in your friendship. Birthdays, holidays, and other significant events are all excellent opportunities to show your appreciation to a friend. A well-chosen gift can enhance the significance of these occasions and make them even more memorable.

Giving gifts to friends can also be a way to express gratitude for their presence in your life. Your friends may have stood by you during difficult times, listened when you needed to vent, or simply been there to make you laugh when you needed it the most. A thoughtful gift can be a great way to say thank you and show how much you appreciate their friendship.

When you give gifts to your friends, you're also demonstrating that you're a thoughtful and considerate person. You're showing that you're aware of their preferences and have taken the time to select a gift that's meaningful to them. This level of consideration is essential in any relationship.

Giving gifts to your friends can also be a way to show support for their hobbies or interests. If your friend is into art, you could give them a set of high-quality paints or brushes. This not only shows that you are interested in their hobbies, but it can also encourage them to pursue their passions and hobbies in the future.

Giving gifts to friends can also be a way to build shared experiences or memories. For example, you could give your friend tickets to a concert or sporting event that you can attend together. This provides a shared experience that you can reflect on in the future.

Another benefit of giving gifts to friends is that it can create a positive environment and spread happiness to those around you. When you provide a gift for someone, it can bring a smile to their face and create a sense of joy and happiness. This can be infectious and spread to those around you, creating a positive atmosphere.

Gift-giving can also be an opportunity to practice creativity and self-expression. When you give a gift to someone, you're putting a part of yourself into the present. It's important to remember that gift-giving should not be about the cost of the gift. A thoughtful, well-chosen gift can be as meaningful as an expensive one.

YOUR MONEY IS YOURS; YOU CHOOSE WHAT YOU DO WITH IT

Your money is yours, and you get to decide what you do with it most of the time. Financial independence and autonomy are essential concepts for you to understand as you get older. You may need to work around a parent or guardian's expectations for saving and spending, but it's highly likely that you have some discretionary income that's purely yours to do with as you wish.

Some people prefer to spend their money on things that provide immediate gratification, such as eating out or buying the newest gadgets. Others may choose to save their money. There's no right or wrong approach, but it's essential to understand the implications of any financial decision.

Financial literacy and education are crucial for making informed financial choices. When you're financially educated, you'll be better prepared to understand the risks and benefits associated with various financial products in the future.

As much as you can do whatever you like with your spending money, you must consciously and intentionally choose. Your teenage years can be exciting and full of opportunities to learn and develop. However, it's also a time when many people make financial mistakes that can have long-term repercussions. From overspending to taking on too much debt when you're 18 or 19, these mistakes can make achieving financial stability in the future challenging. Be smart with your money and make wise financial choices that will benefit you in the long run.

Here are some common money mistakes that you should take care to avoid:

Credit Card Debt

Credit cards can be a valuable tool for managing money and building credit, but they can also be a trap if you're not familiar with how they work. Credit card debt can quickly spiral out of control, leaving you with high interest rates and a damaged credit score.

Use your credit card only for necessary expenses, and make sure to pay it off in full each month. If you're carrying a balance, make sure to pay more than the minimum payment each month to avoid paying high interest.

Overspending on Unnecessary Items

Overspending on unnecessary things is one of the most common money mistakes teenagers make. From designer clothing to the newest gadgets, it's all too easy to get caught up in the hype and overspend.

Instead of buying a new outfit every week, try to find ways to mix and match the clothes you already own. If you're tempted to buy a new gadget, do some research and make sure it's something you really need before making the purchase.

Borrowing Money You Can't Repay

It's crucial to avoid borrowing money that you won't be able to repay. This includes using a credit card to pay for unaffordable expenses or borrowing money from friends or family. If you must borrow money, make sure you have a repayment plan in place. Prior to taking even an unofficial loan from friends, make a budget that includes your monthly payments and make sure you can afford them. Being unable to repay money you owe to a friend could strain your relationships and undo all the progress you've made while working on your social skills.

CHAPTER ELEVEN: BULLYING

Do you know what bullying is and why it happens? Bullying is when someone repeatedly and intentionally harms another person or a group of people who are unable to defend themselves. It can take many forms, including physical violence, verbal abuse, and emotional manipulation. Bullying can happen in different places, including school, online spaces, or even at work. It's important to know that bullying isn't just a normal part of growing up, and it can have severe consequences for both the victim and the bully.

Unfortunately, bullying is a widespread problem in our society. You might have seen it happen in movies or even experienced it in real life. For example, a bully might push another person or call them hurtful names. Other types of bullying are less obvious and less talked about.

Bullies might justify their actions, but it usually comes down to a desire for power and control over others. They might also think that making someone else feel bad will make them feel better about themselves.

In this chapter, we'll explore what bullying is and why people engage in it. It's important for people to understand bullying so that they can work to stop it and create a safer, more respectful environment for everyone.

Why Do People Bully Others?

If you've ever been bullied, you may wonder why some people act in such hurtful ways. Understanding why bullies behave as they do can help you recognize the signs and learn how to protect yourself or others from harm. While there's never an excuse for this type of behavior, there are several common reasons why some teenagers choose to bully others.

Power: Bullies often want to feel powerful or authoritative. Adolescents who feel powerless or have low self-esteem may use bullying as a way to gain control over others. They may turn to bullying if they think they cannot get what they want through positive social interactions. Boys and girls are equally likely to engage in relational aggression such as gossiping or exclusion to gain social dominance.

Popularity: Another reason why some teenagers may bully others is to gain popularity or social standing. Bullies may target less popular peers or spread rumors and gossip to gain attention from others. This can be especially true for adolescents who are trying to climb the social ladder or gain social power. They may see bullying as a way to trample on others in order to elevate their own status.

Payback: Some bullied teenagers may also turn to bullying as a form of payback or revenge. These individuals, often referred to as "bully victims," may feel that their actions are justified because they too have been hurt or bullied by others. They may lash out, often at those who are weaker or more vulnerable, to regain a sense of power or control.

Domestic issues: Some teenagers may turn to bullying because of issues in their home or family lives. Adolescents who grow up in abusive households may turn to bullying as a way to feel powerful or in control. Additionally, siblings who bully one another may learn to use bullying to exert control over others.

Pleasure: Sadly, some teenagers may bully others simply because it gives them pleasure. These individuals may enjoy hurting others and find humor in their victim s pain. They may lack empathy or be driven by a desire for attention or entertainment. These types of bullies can be particularly dangerous because they might not see any reason to stop their behavior.

117

Prejudices: Some teenagers may bully others because of prejudices or biases they hold. Bullies may target marginalized individuals based on their ethnicity, religion, gender identity, or sexual orientation.

Regardless of the reasons behind bullying, it's important to remember that this behavior is never justified. If you or someone you know is being bullied, seek help and support from a trusted adult such as a teacher, counselor, or parent. Additionally, resources such as hotlines and online support groups can provide valuable information and support.

If you feel that you may be a bully, it's time to reflect on your actions and try to understand what's causing you to hurt others. It may be helpful to seek counseling or talk to a trusted adult about your feelings and experiences. Remember that it's never too late to change your behavior and make amends for the harm you've caused.

How to Spot Bullying Behavior

You need to able to identify bullying behavior in order to take preventative measures. Here are some typical signs that a bully may normally exhibit:

- Physical aggression or brutality
- Verbal slander or slurs
- Disseminating hearsay or gossip
- Ostracizing or excluding others

- Attacking people on social media or other internet platforms

If someone you know exhibits any of these behaviors, alert an adult for guidance before the situation can escalate.

How to Defend Yourself Without Resorting to Violence

You may have heard that violence is never the answer, and that's especially true when it comes to self-defense. It can be tempting to lash out physically when facing a bully, but it's much better to rely on nonviolent methods. Here are some great ways to protect yourself without resorting to violence:

Stay calm: First off, ignoring a bully can be a powerful tool. Bullies want to get a reaction out of you, so if you don't give them one, they may lose interest. It takes a lot of strength to stay calm and not respond, but it can be one of the most effective ways to avoid a physical fight.

Use humor: Humor can be a powerful weapon against bullies. If you can respond to their taunts with a clever joke or a witty remark, you might catch them off guard and make them think twice about continuing to pick on you. After all, if you can disarm them with words, there's no need to get physical.

Stand tall: Body language is another key factor in self-defense. If you stand tall, maintain eye contact, and avoid slouching or looking down, you'll give off an air of confidence that might make bullies think twice about targeting you.

Develop a support system: It's also important to have a support system in place. Surround yourself with friends and family members who make you feel safe and supported. They can help you cope with bullying and provide emotional support when you need it.

Assert yourself: Being assertive is another effective way to defend yourself. Practice saying no confidently and firmly and be clear about what behavior you will and will not accept from others. If you're outspoken and stand up for yourself, bullies may be less likely to bother you.

How to Speak Up and Seek Help

It's crucial to speak up and get help if you're being bullied. It might be challenging to do, but it's necessary to break the cycle of abuse and regain control. Let's explore some ways to seek help and speak up when you're bullied.

Ask for help: First off, it's essential to understand that you can achieve a lot on your own. It might be difficult to ask for help when you feel vulnerable or ashamed, but it's okay to seek assistance. Nobody deserves to be bullied, and you deserve to feel safe and protected. Asking for help doesn't make you weak; it makes you powerful and in control.

Talk to an adult: Find someone you trust. It could be a parent, teacher, counselor, or coach. Having someone who can offer advice and support is crucial. Talk to them about what's been happening and how you're feeling. They can help you come up with a plan to deal with the situation and protect yourself.

Document the details: Keep a record of each bullying incident. Write down the dates, times, and details of what happened. This can be helpful when you're asking for help because it provides concrete evidence of what's going on. Jot down notes in a notebook or on your phone whenever something happens.

Be honest about your mental health: Seek professional help if you're struggling with the effects of bullying on your mental health. A counselor or therapist can help you process your emotions and develop coping strategies. They can also provide additional support and guidance as you deal with bullying.

Remember that you're not alone and there's always someone willing to help. Don't be afraid to speak up and seek assistance when you need it.

CHAPTER TWELVE: MENTAL HEALTH

Mental health refers to your psychological and emotional well-being. It's all about being able to control your emotions and behaviors, handle stress, make choices, and have healthy relationships with others.

A lot of things can affect your mental health, including your genes, environment, experiences, and physical health. Conditions such as depression or anxiety can affect your thoughts, emotions, and behavior, and they can make it hard to function in your day-to-day life.

That's why it's very important to take care of your mental health. You can do this by practicing self-care, seeking professional help when needed, and surrounding yourself with people and environments that support positive mental health. Mental health is just as important as your physical health! Take care of yourself and reach out for help if you need it.

If you're struggling with symptoms of a mental health condition that interfere with your daily life, you should seek professional help instead of trying to manage them on your own. A mental health specialist can help you identify your specific condition and offer treatment options to manage your symptoms and improve your overall mental health. Don't be afraid to reach out for help!

How Does Anxiety Affect Social Skills?

Anxiety is when you feel worried, nervous, or uneasy because of an actual or perceived threat or danger. It's a common feeling that everyone experiences from time to time, but when it becomes excessive or overwhelming, it can interfere with your everyday activities and affect your quality of life.

There are different things that can cause anxiety, such as stress, uncertainty, or fear. Some typical signs of anxiety include a racing heart, sweaty palms, shortness of breath, restlessness, and trouble focusing. Physical symptoms such as headaches, stomachaches, and muscular tension can also happen because of anxiety.

If you're feeling anxious, you're not alone. There are many ways to manage anxiety, such as practicing relaxation techniques, seeking support from loved ones, visiting a mental health professional, and doing activities that you find enjoyable and calming. It's important to know that anxiety can make it difficult to be social.

One type of anxiety is social anxiety disorder. This is when you feel really afraid of being judged or embarrassed in social settings. It can make it difficult to participate in social activities or engage in conversations with others. But don't worry; there are ways to manage this condition with therapy and medication.

Another type of anxiety is generalized anxiety disorder. This is when you worry excessively about daily events and activities. You might be overly concerned about social obligations like meeting new people or giving a presentation, and it can cause you to avoid these situations entirely. Again, therapy and medication can be helpful in managing this condition.

Panic disorder is another type of anxiety; it is marked by unexpected and sudden panic attacks. You might feel intense fear and physical symptoms like rapid heartbeat, sweating, and trembling. This can make social settings overwhelming, but treatment can help you learn to manage these attacks.

If you're experiencing signs of a mental health condition that are interfering with your ability to participate in social activities or interact with others, it's critical that you seek professional assistance. A mental health expert can provide an accurate diagnosis and work with you to create a treatment plan.

How to Practice Being Less Anxious

Anxiety can be a debilitating condition that negatively impacts all aspects of a person's life, including their relationships, work, and personal well-being. While anxiety can be challenging to manage, there are several ways to practice being less anxious that can help reduce symptoms. Common strategies include mindfulness techniques, self-care, cognitive behavioral therapy (CBT), and medication.

Identifying Triggers

The first step in dealing with anxiety is to determine what causes it. Keeping a journal and recording the circumstances or thoughts that make you anxious can help you recognize patterns and develop strategies to cope with them. For example, if having too much on your plate makes you anxious, consider prioritizing chores and breaking them down into smaller, manageable chunks.

Mindfulness Techniques

Mindfulness is the practice of being present in the moment and aware of your thoughts and emotions without judgment. By learning to be mindful, you can become more aware of your anxious thoughts and feelings and learn to accept them without getting caught up in them. This can help you reduce the impact of anxiety in your life and feel more in control of your emotions.

Some effective mindfulness techniques include:

Breathing exercises: Focusing on your breath and taking slow, deep breaths can help to calm your mind and reduce anxiety.

Meditation: Meditation can reduce stress and improve your overall well-being. You can start with just a few minutes of meditation each day and gradually increase the time as you become more comfortable with the practice.

Yoga: Yoga is a physical and mental practice that combines movement, breathing, and meditation. It can be an effective way to reduce anxiety.

Self-Care

Self-care is an essential component of managing anxiety. Practicing self-care can help you reduce stress, improve your mood, and increase your overall sense of well-being. Some effective self-care strategies include:

Exercise: Regular exercise can reduce anxiety by releasing endorphins and improving overall physical health. You don't have to engage in intense workouts to experience the benefits of exercise; even a daily walk or yoga session can be helpful.

A healthy diet: Try to incorporate plenty of fruits, vegetables, whole grains, and lean protein into your diet. Limit your intake of processed and sugary foods.

Sleep: Try to establish a regular sleep routine and create a sleep-friendly environment by keeping your bedroom cool and dark.

Relaxation techniques: Engaging in relaxation techniques, such as taking a warm bath, reading a book, or listening to calming music can reduce anxiety.

Cognitive Behavioral Therapy

Cognitive behavioral therapy is often used to treat anxiety. CBT is a short-term, goal-oriented therapy that focuses on changing negative thoughts and behaviors that contribute to anxiety. CBT can help you identify and challenge negative beliefs and replace them with more positive and realistic ones. It can also help you develop coping strategies for managing anxiety as you continue to develop your social skills.

Some techniques used in CBT include:

Thought challenging: This involves identifying and challenging negative thoughts with more positive and realistic ones.

Exposure therapy: This involves gradually exposing yourself to situations that trigger anxiety in a safe and controlled environment to help you become desensitized to them.

Relaxation training: This involves learning relaxation techniques such as deep breathing and progressive muscle relaxation.

Deep Breathing

Deep breathing is a simple yet effective method for dealing with anxiety. When you feel anxious, take a few deep breaths, inhaling deeply through your nostrils and exhaling slowly through your mouth. Deep breathing activates the parasympathetic nervous system, which is responsible for relaxation, and deactivates the sympathetic nervous system, which is responsible for the fight-or-flight response. By practicing deep breathing regularly, you can train your body to respond more calmly to stressful situations.

Positive Affirmations

Negative affirmation or saying negative things can make anxiety worse. Instead, practice positive affirmation. Remind yourself of your strengths and accomplishments and focus on the positive aspects of your life.

How to Seek Assistance

Unfortunately, seeking care for mental health can be overwhelming. Many people are reluctant to seek help because of stigma, fear of judgment, or a lack of information about available resources. However, mental health issues are common and treatable, and seeking help will allow you to feel better and improve your quality of life.

If you're struggling with mental health issues and want to seek help, there are several ways to pursue confidential, affordable, and effective mental health care. Here are some tips on how to obtain mental health help:

Acknowledge That You Need Help

The first step in seeking mental health assistance is to acknowledge that you need help. This might be difficult, but it's an essential starting point.

Consult Your Family Doctor

If you're not sure where to start, talk to your family doctor. They can assess your symptoms and refer you to a mental health specialist if necessary. Your doctor can also prescribe medication or provide other treatments, such as therapy or counseling. Depending on your age, you may or may not need to involve your parents or guardians in this part of the process.

Seek Recommendations from Trusted Sources

If speaking with your doctor makes you uncomfortable, you can reach out to trusted family members, friends, or peers. They may be familiar with mental health specialists in your community or otherwise able to offer advice based on their personal experiences.

Use Online Resources

The internet has made things somewhat easier these days. There are many online resources available to help you find mental health assistance. Websites such as Psychology Today, GoodTherapy, and the National

Alliance on Mental Illness (NAMI) offer directories of mental health providers in your area.

Contact Your Insurance Provider

If you have health insurance, your parent or guardian may need to contact your insurance provider to find out what mental health services are covered under your plan. Many insurance plans offer coverage for mental health services, including therapy and counseling.

Look for Low-Cost Options

There are several low-cost options if you don't have health insurance or can't afford mental health services. In addition to the free or low-cost mental health services provided by many neighborhood mental health centers, some universities and colleges also provide counseling to their student populations. You can also search for therapists who give their services on a sliding scale based on your ability to pay.

Choose a Mental Health Specialist Who Fits Your Needs

It's crucial to pick a mental health professional who matches your requirements when making this decision. Think about things like their training, experience, and area of expertise. You might also want to think about how they handle treatment. Some specialists might emphasize talk therapy, while others might prescribe medication or use alternative therapies.

Schedule an Appointment

As soon as you've found a mental health professional who suits your requirements, schedule an appointment. Many service providers provide free initial consultations, which can be a useful way to learn more about their philosophy and assess whether they're a good match for you.

Be Open and Honest

When you speak with your mental health professional, be open and honest about your symptoms and worries. This will enable them to offer the finest care and assistance. Remember that your mental health professional is there to assist you and that getting treatment for mental health problems isn't a shameful thing to do.

CONCLUSION

As you come to the end of this book, hopefully you have found useful information and helpful insights about how to develop social skills during this time in your life. Remember that your teenage years can be challenging, but they can also be exciting and fulfilling. With the proper guidance and support, you can navigate this phase of your life with confidence and emerge as a strong and empowered young adult.

Throughout this book, we've covered financial discipline, socializing, communication, setting boundaries and balancing responsibilities, and seeking help when needed. These are all important skills that will serve you well not just in your teenage years but throughout your life.

One key takeaway from this book is that it's okay to ask for help as you set out to make new friends and strengthen your social relationships. At this stage in your life, you're still learning and growing, and there will be times when you need support from others. Asking for help isn't a sign of weakness; it's a sign of strength and self-awareness. Remember that there are people in your life who care about you and want to help you succeed, whether that's your parents, friends, or teachers.

Another key theme in this book is the importance of setting boundaries. Learning to say no and stand up for yourself is a crucial skill that will serve you well in all areas of your life, from your personal relationships to your academic and professional pursuits. Remember that your time and energy are valuable, and it's okay to prioritize your own needs and goals.

Of course, the teenage years are also a time when many young people experience bullying or other forms of mistreatment. It's important to recognize that bullying is never okay and to know how to seek help if you're being targeted. There are resources available to you, including school counselors, teachers, and hotlines, and you shouldn't be afraid to speak up if you or someone you know is being bullied.

As you move forward into young adulthood, remember to stay true to yourself and your values. It's easy to get caught up in peer pressure or societal expectations, but ultimately, you are the one who has to live with the choices you make. Take the time to figure out who you are and what you stand for, and don't be afraid to pursue your passions and interests, even if they are different from those of your peers.

Finally, remember that your teenage years are just the beginning of your journey through life. There will be ups and downs, successes and failures, but each experience will help you grow and learn. Embrace the challenges and opportunities that come your way, and never stop striving to be the best version of yourself.

There are people in your life who care about you and want to see you thrive. With the right mindset and support, you can overcome any obstacle and achieve your goals. Good luck on your journey, and remember to always stay true to yourself.